Landmarks of wor

Thomas Mann

DOCTOR FAUSTUS

Landmarks of world literature

General editor: J. P. Stern

THOMAS MANN

Doctor Faustus

MICHAEL BEDDOW
Professor of German, University of Leeds

CAMBRIDGE
UNIVERSITY PRESS

Published by the Press Syndicate of the University of Cambridge
The Pitt Building, Trumpington Street, Cambridge CB2 1RP
40 West 20th Street, New York NY 10011-4211, USA
10 Stamford Road, Oakleigh, Melbourne 3166, Australia

First published 1994

A catalogue record for this book is available from the British Library

Library of Congress cataloguing in publication data
Beddow, Michael.
Thomas Mann, Doctor Faustus / Michael Beddow.
    p.   cm. – (Landmarks of world literature)
ISBN 0 521 37575 4 (hardback) / ISBN 0 521 37592 4 (paperback)
1. Mann, Thomas, 1875–1955. Doctor Faustus. I. Title.
II. Series.
PT2625.A44D6889   1994
823'.912 – dc20   93-49364 CIP

ISBN 0 521 37575 4 hardback
ISBN 0 521 37592 4 paperback

Transferred to digital printing 2004

WG

In memoriam

Joseph Peter Maria Stern

Contents

Acknowledgements

This book could not have been written without the facilities of the Institute of Germanic Studies in London and of Cambridge University Library. I must also record my gratitude to my former colleagues, the Master and Fellows of Trinity Hall, for their hospitality and intellectual support, and to the engineers and programmers responsible for the Internet, which brought the world's library catalogues to my desk.

This was one of the last manuscripts to pass through the hands of the series editor, Peter Stern. What I owe to him is inexpressible. He deserves a far better memorial than I can provide, but nonetheless I offer this book to his memory, in mourning and gratitude.

Leeds 1992
Michael Beddow

Chronology of Thomas Mann's life and works

	Thomas Mann's life and works	Literary and cultural events	Historical events
1871	Birth of Heinrich, Thomas Mann's elder brother.	Nietzsche, *The Birth of Tragedy.*	Proclamation of German Empire.
1875	Thomas Mann born (6 June).		
1883		Wagner dies.	
1889	Enters secondary school.	Hauptmann, *Before Sunrise.* Ibsen, *Ghosts.* Nietzsche collapses into insanity.	
1890	100th anniversary of Mann family firm.		Bismarck dismissed as Chancellor.
1891	Death of father. Winding up of firm.	Wedekind, *Spring's Awakening.* Mahler, *First Symphony.*	
1892		Hauptmann, *The Weavers.* Ibsen, *The Master Builder.*	
1894	Move to Munich. Trainee in insurance office and occasional student at University. *Gefallen.*		
1895		Fontane, *Effi Briest.* Röntgen discovers X-rays.	Kiel Canal opened.
1896	To Rome and Palestrina with Heinrich.		

1897	*Buddenbrooks* begun.	Fontane, *Der Stechlin*. Chekhov, *Uncle Vanya*. Brahms dies.	
1898	Return from Italy to Munich.	Fontane dies. Bismarck dies. Discovery of Radium (Curies).	
1899		Freud, *The Interpretation of Dreams* (dated 1900). Ibsen, *When We Dead Awaken*.	Boer War (–1902).
1900	(Curtailed) military service.	Conrad, *Lord Jim*. Bergson, *Le Rire*. Nietzsche dies. Max Planck's quantum theory.	
1901	*Buddenbrooks*.	Chekhov, *Three Sisters*. Nietzsche, *Der Wille zur Macht*, *Nietzsche contra Wagner*.	
1902		Conrad, *Heart of Darkness*. Gide, *L'Immoraliste*. Zola dies.	
1903	*Tonio Kröger*.	Weininger, *Geschlecht und Charakter*. Schoenberg, *Gurrelieder*.	
1904	Engagement to Katja Pringsheim.	Wedekind, *Pandora's Box*. James, *The Golden Bowl*. Conrad, *Nostromo*. Chekhov, *The Cherry Orchard*. Romain Rolland, *Jean Christophe* (–1912). Freud, *The Psychopathology of Everyday Life*. Richard Strauss, *Salome*.	*Entente cordiale* between Britain and France.

1905	*Fiorenza* (Mann's only play), Marriage. First notes for *Faustus* project.	H. Mann, *Professor Unrat*. Musil, *Young Törless*. Unamuno, *Life of Don Quixote and Sancho*. Max Weber, *The Protestant Ethic and the Rise of Capitalism*. Debussy, *La Mer*. Einstein's special theory of relativity.	Abortive revolution in Russia.
1908		Sorel, *Réflexions sur la violence*. Rilke, *Neue Gedichte II*. Mahler, *Das Lied von der Erde*. Webern, *Passacaglia*.	
1909	*Royal Highness*.	Marinetti, *Manifeste du futurisme*. Schoenberg, *Erwartung*.	
1910	Suicide of Clara, Mann's younger sister.	E. M. Forster, *Howards End*. Russell and Whitehead, *Principia Mathematica I*. Stravinsky, *The Firebird*. Tolstoy dies.	
1911		Hofmannsthal, *Der Rosenkavalier*, *Jedermann*. Pound, *Canzoni*. Schoenberg, *Pierrot Lunaire*. Rutherford's nuclear theory of the atom. Mahler dies.	
1912	*Death in Venice*.	Benn, *Morgue*. Hofmannsthal, *Ariadne auf Naxos*. Strindberg dies.	*Titanic* sinks.

1913	*The Magic Mountain* begun.	Kafka, *The Judgement.* Apollinaire, *Alcools.* Proust, *Du Côté de chez Swann.* Unamuno, *The Tragic Sense of Life.* Freud, *Totem und Tabu.* Husserl, *Phenomenologie.* Stravinsky, *The Rite of Spring.* Einstein's General Theory of Relativity. Bohr's theory of atomic structure.	
1914	*Gedanken im Kriege.* Beginning of rift with Heinrich.	Gide, *Les Caves du Vatican.* Joyce, *Dubliners.*	First World War begins.
1915	*Frederick the Great and the Grand Coalition. Reflections of a Nonpolitical Man* begun.	H. Mann, *Zola.* Romain Rolland, *Au-dessus de la mêlée.* Ford Madox Ford, *The Good Soldier.*	Sinking of the *Lusitania* by German U-boat.
1916		Kafka, *Metamorphosis.* James Joyce, *Portrait of the Artist as a Young Man.* Jung, *The Psychology of the Unconscious.* Henry James dies.	
1917		Eliot, *Prufrock.* Valéry, *La Jeune Parque.* Dada launched in Zürich (Cabaret Voltaire).	USA enters the war. October revolution in Russia. Armistice on Russian front.

1918	Reflections of a Nonpolitical Man.	H. Mann, Der Untertan (Man of Straw). Proust, A l'Ombre des jeunes filles en fleurs. Spengler, The Decline of the West I. Stravinsky, The Soldier's Tale. Debussy dies. Rutherford splits the atom.	Revolution and abdication of Emperor, proclamation of Republic, Armistice.
1919	The Magic Mountain resumed. Honorary doctorate from Bonn University.	Gide, La Symphonie pastorale. Kafka, A Country Doctor, In the Penal Colony. Kraus, Die letzten Tage der Menschheit.	Spartakus uprising in Berlin: assassination of Paul Liebknecht and Rosa Luxemburg. Soviet Republic in Munich. Treaty of Versailles. Weimar Constitution.
1920			Kapp's Putsch in Berlin brought down by general strike. Suppression of left-wing governments in Ruhr district.
1921	Goethe and Tolstoi.	Proust, Sodome et Gomorrhe (–1923). Pirandello, Six Characters in Search of an Author. First Donaueschingen Festival of New Music.	
1922	Reconciliation with Heinrich. Declaration of support for Republic.	Brecht, Baal, Trommeln in der Nacht. Joyce, Ulysses. T. S. Eliot, The Waste Land.	Assassination of Reich Foreign Minister Rathenau. Mussolini's march on Rome.

1922 *cont'd*	Valéry, *Charmes.* Pirandello, *Henry IV.* Bergson, *Durée et simultanéité.* Spengler, *The Decline of the West II.* Wittgenstein, *Tractatus Logico-Philosophicus.* Proust dies.	
1923	Rilke, *Duino Elegies, Sonnets to Orpheus.* Proust, *La Prisonnière.* Svevo, *La coscienza di Zeno.*	Hyperinflation in Germany. French occupation of Ruhr district. Hitler's abortive Putsch in Munich. USSR established.
1924	*The Magic Mountain.*	Kafka, *A Hunger Artist.* E. M. Forster, *A Passage to India.* Breton, *Surrealist Manifesto.* Kafka dies. Conrad dies.	Lenin dies, rise of Stalin, banishment of Trotsky. Stabilisation of the German mark.
1925	*Joseph* begun.	Kafka, *The Trial.* John Dos Passos, *Manhattan Transfer.* Fitzgerald, *The Great Gatsby.* Virginia Woolf, *Mrs Dalloway.* Proust, *Albertine disparue.* Adolf Hitler, *Mein Kampf.* Alban Berg, *Wozzeck.*	Hindenburg elected German President.
1926		Kafka, *The Castle.* Gide, *Les Faux-Monnayeurs.*	Germany admitted to League of Nations.

1927	Hesse, *Steppenwolf*. V. Woolf, *To the Lighthouse*. Heidegger, *Being and Time*.	
1928	Brecht/Weill, *Threepenny Opera*. Schoenberg, *Variations for Orchestra*. Webern, *Symphony*. Ravel, *Bolero*.	
1929	*Mario and the Magician*. Nobel Prize for Literature.	Döblin, *Berlin Alexanderplatz*. Remarque, *All Quiet on the Western Front*. Hemingway, *A Farewell to Arms*. Thomas Wolfe, *Look Homeward, Angel*. Hofmannsthal dies.	Wall Street crash, world economic crisis destabilises Weimar Republic.
1930	*Deutsche Ansprache*.	Musil, *The Man Without Qualities I*. T.S. Eliot, *Ash Wednesday*. Freud, *Civilisation and its Discontents*. D.H. Lawrence dies.	Large electoral gains by National Socialists. 4.4 million unemployed in Germany.
1932		Ernst Jünger, *Der Arbeiter*. Aldous Huxley, *Brave New World*. Stravinsky, *Symphony of Psalms*.	6 million unemployed in Germany.
1933	*Sufferings and Greatness of Richard Wagner*. Exile begins. *The Stories of Jacob* (Vol. I of *Joseph and his Brothers*).		Hitler becomes Reich Chancellor. Reichstag fire. Concordat with Vatican. Enabling Law gives Hitler dictatorial powers.

1933 *cont'd*		Banning of political parties and trade unions. Emigration of many artists and intellectuals. Public book-burnings.
1934	*The Young Joseph.* First visit to USA.	Hindemith, *Mathis der Maler.*	Elimination of SA by SS, murder of large number of Hitler's opponents. Assassination of Austrian Chancellor Dollfuß.
1935		Berg, *Violin Concerto.*	Nuremberg racial legislation.
1936	Attack on National Socialism in published correspondence over withdrawal of honorary doctorate by University of Bonn. *Joseph in Egypt.* *Lotte in Weimar* begun.	Schoenberg, *Violin Concerto.*	Spanish Civil War (–1939). Moscow Show Trials (–1938). Hitler remilitarises Rhineland. Berlin–Rome Axis established. Olympic Games in Berlin.
1937		Carl Orff, *Carmina Burana.* Alban Berg, *Lulu.*	Exhibition of 'Degenerate Art' tours German cities.
1938	Decision to move to USA. Public criticism of Appeasement.	Sartre, *La Nausée.* First artificial fission of uranium (Hahn/Straßmann/Meitner).	Anschluß of Austria. Munich agreement. November Pogroms.
1939	Lecturer in the Humanities at Princeton. *Lotte in Weimar.*	Ernst Jünger, *Auf den Marmorklippen.* Steinbeck, *The Grapes of Wrath.*	Fascist victory in Spanish Civil War. Hitler-Stalin-Pact. German attack on Poland begins Second World War.
1940	Monthly broadcasts to Germany (–1945).	Hemingway, *For Whom the Bell Tolls.* Graham Greene, *The Power and the Glory.* Suicide of Walter Benjamin.	German occupation of Denmark, Norway, France. Churchill becomes British Prime Minister. British retreat from Dunkirk. Battle of Britain.

1941	Move to California.	Brecht, *Mother Courage.*	German invasion of Soviet Union, North Africa campaign. Japanese attack on Pearl Harbor brings USA into war.
1942	*Joseph* completed.	Brecht, *Life of Galileo.* Camus, *L'Etranger.* Schoenberg, *Piano Concerto.* Musil dies.	Lidice destroyed as reprisal for assassination of Heydrich. Wannsee-Conference plans 'Final Solution of the Jewish Problem'. First nuclear chain reaction (Fermi).
1943	*Doctor Faustus* begun. Friendship with Adorno.	Hesse, *The Glass Beads Game.* Sartre, *Les Mouches.*	German defeat at Stalingrad. Afrika-Korps surrenders. Fall of Mussolini, allied landings in Italy. Heavy air raids on German cities. 'White Rose' resistance group in Munich.
1944	US citizenship. Campaign speech for F.D. Roosevelt.	Sartre, *Huis clos.*	Allied landings in Normandy. Assassination attempt on Hitler (20 July). Warsaw uprising. German troops retreat to Reich frontiers. V2 rockets against England.
1945	Controversy with representatives of 'inner emigration'.		Suicide of Hitler, Goebbels, Himmler. Unconditional surrender of Germany. Atomic bombs on Hiroshima and Nagasaki, surrender of Japan. Germany divided into four occupation zones. War-crime trials (–1948).

1946	Successful operation for lung cancer.	Severe food shortages in occupied Germany. Black-market economy.
1947	*Doctor Faustus* completed. *Nietzsche's Philosophy in the Light of Our Experience.* Trip to Europe (London, Switzerland, Holland). Continuing controversy about 'inner emigration'.	Zuckmayer, *The Devil's General.* Hauptmann dies.	Borchert, *Draußen vor der Tür.* Formation of Gruppe 47. Camus, *La Peste.* Adorno/Horkheimer, *Dialektik der Aufklärung.*	US and British occupation zones merged. Beginning of US economic aid for Western Europe (Marshall Plan).
1948	*'Doctor Faustus'. The Genesis of a Novel.*	Brecht, *The Caucasian Chalk Circle.* Brecht moves to East Berlin. Mailer, *The Naked and the Dead.* Sartre, *Les Mains sales.*	Soviet blockade of West Berlin, Western Allies mount airlift. Communist takeover in Czechoslovakia. French occupation zone fused with former British and American zones. Currency reform stabilises economy.
1949	Second post-war European trip, including Germany. Public appearances in Frankfurt und Weimar. Suicide of eldest son, Klaus.	George Orwell, *1984.*	Foundation of NATO. Establishment of German Federal Republic, German Democratic Republic, People's Republic of China.
1950	H. Mann dies.	Ionesco, *The Bald Prima-Donna.*	Korean War (–1953). McCarthyism in USA.
1951		Adorno, *Minima Moralia.* Simone de Beauvoir, *Le Deuxième Sexe.* Schoenberg dies.	Alfred Krupp's war-crimes sentence commuted and his property restored.

1952	Moves to Switzerland.	Hemingway, *The Old Man and the Sea*.	American hydrogen bomb tests.
1953	*Felix Krull*.	Steinbeck, *East of Eden*. Böll, *Und sagte kein einziges Wort*.	Death of Stalin. June Uprising in GDR. USSR has hydrogen bomb. Partitioning of Korea.
1954	*Essay on Chekhov*.	Max Frisch, *Stiller*. Böll, *Haus ohne Hüter*. William Golding, *Lord of the Flies*.	French defeat at Dien Bien Phu, partitioning of Vietnam. Federal Republic joins NATO.
1955	*Essay on Schiller*. Dies 12 August.	Böll, *Das Brot der frühen Jahre*. Herbert Marcuse, *Eros and Civilisation*.	Warsaw Pact established. Britain to build hydrogen bombs. Saarland votes to return to German rule.

Chronology of Adrian Leverkühn's life and works

	Life	*Works*
1885	Born at Oberweiler, near Weißenfels in Saxony.	
1895	Lodges with uncle in Kaisersaschern while attending grammar school.	
1899	Starts music lessons with Wendel Kretzschmar.	
1903	Study of theology at Halle University.	
1905–10	Study of composition at Leipzig. Syphilitic infection.	*Meerleuchten*, orchestral piece in the manner of Debussy. Verlaine and Blake Lieder. Brentano song-cycle (first serial experiments). Dante settings.
1910	Moves to Munich. Lodges with the Rodde family.	Opera, *Love's Labour's Lost* begun.
1911	Stay in Italy (Rome and Palestrina) with Rüdiger Schildknapp. Dialogue with the devil.	
1912	Return to Germany: takes up residence at Schweigestills' farm in Pfeiffering, near Munich.	*Love's Labour's Lost* completed.
1913		Settings of Blake and Keats. *Frühlingsfeyer* for baritone, organ and string orchestra.
1914		*Wonders of the Universe*, fantasia for orchestra in one movement. *Gesta Romanorum*, opera for puppets.

1919		*Apocalipsis cum figuris*, oratorio.
1924	Visits Schloß Tolna (Hungary) with Rudi Schwerdtfeger: beginning of their intimacy.	*Violin Concerto.*
1925	Proposes marriage via Rudi Schwerdtfeger to Marie Godeau.	
1927		*Music for strings, woodwind and piano.* *String quartet.* *Trio for violin, viola and cello.*
1928	Visit and death of his nephew Nepomuk ('Echo').	*Ariel's Songs* from *The Tempest.*
1930	Mental collapse. Taken back by mother to family farm.	*The Lamentation of Dr Faustus*, choral symphony.
1940	Death.	

Editions and references

All references to Thomas Mann's works are to *Werke in 13 Bänden* (Frankfurt am Main, 1974). *Doktor Faustus* is in volume VI, and references to this original text of the novel are by page number alone, followed by a page reference, preceded by the letters LP, to the corresponding passage in the English translation by Helen Lowe-Porter, in the edition published by Everyman's Library (London, 1992). The translations given are, however, my own. For all other works by Mann, the volume number in roman figures precedes the page number. References to Nietzsche's works are to *Werke in 3 Bänden*, edited by K. Schlechta (Munich, 1960), and those to Adorno's *Philosophie der neuen Musik* (abbreviated *PdnM*) to the Suhrkamp paperback edition (Frankfurt am Main, 1978). Here, too, the translations of passages quoted are my own.

Chapter 1

Antecedents

Biography

Thomas Mann was born into a family of grain merchants in the Baltic seaport of Lübeck in 1875, four years after the proclamation of the German Empire. His childhood coincided with the 'Gründerjahre' of the new united Germany, marked by rapid industrial and commercial expansion. His father died suddenly when Thomas was sixteen, leaving a will which wound up the family firm, whereupon his mother took the family to Munich, at that time the artistic and cultural centre of the new Reich.

Thomas, who had never shown any academic prowess or interest in a conventional profession, worked for a while in an insurance firm and enrolled for various university courses; most of his time, though, was spent in what would later figure in *Doctor Faustus* as the 'house-trained Bohemian' circles of the Bavarian capital. His first story, 'Gefallen' (Fallen: 1894) appeared when he was nineteen, but the real foundation of his career was the publication in 1897 of *Little Herr Friedemann*. On the strength of this novella, Samuel Fischer, a leading progressive publisher, suggested he should try his hand at a larger-scale narrative. The result was *Buddenbrooks* (begun 1897, finished 1900), a novel drawing extensively on his family history, through which Thomas Mann taught himself the craft of fiction in the grand manner. It was partly written during a stay in Italy in the company of his elder brother and fellow aspiring novelist Heinrich, including a summer in Palestrina in the house that was later to provide the setting for Adrian Leverkühn's encounter with the devil. The success of *Buddenbrooks* opened many doors, and in 1905 Mann married Katja Pringsheim, a banker's daughter. Through art he had regained the financial and social position of his merchant forbears.

Before 1914 Mann's fiction was largely concerned with identity conflicts in characters torn between artistic adventure and bourgeois propriety. The novellas *Tristan* (1903), *Tonio Kröger* (1903) and *Death in Venice* (1912) all explore this theme, as does the short novel *Royal Highness* (1909), though the tone and treatment are as varied as the essential theme is uniform. The plot of *Buddenbrooks* is set against the background of Prussia's rise to hegemony over the other German states, and European political crises receive a passing mention in the opening sentence of *Death in Venice*; but otherwise Mann showed no interest in political affairs until war broke out in 1914, sweeping him up into the euphoria which gripped most of Europe's intellectuals. From his fortieth year to his death, Mann's development as a writer was significantly shaped by political forces and events. Engagement with the major issues of the day eventually became part of his own self-understanding, culminating in the *Faustus* project, his attempt at a fictional summation and evaluation of his own creative career and of his nation's role in modern European history and culture.

Mann's enthusiasm for the war stemmed from his belief that it meant the end of the decadent fin-de-siècle culture which had nourished the dilemmas of his principal characters. Commitment to the national cause, viewed as a fight to establish a revitalised nation in a social and political framework appropriate to the German national character, was the tenor of Mann's first political publication, 'Gedanken im Kriege' (Thoughts in Wartime) of September 1914. But Mann's ironic temperament could not sustain such brash simplicities for long. His essay 'Friedrich und die große Koalition' (Frederick the Great and the Grand Coalition: 1915) draws on the psychology of decadence to portray Frederick as an activist aesthete, motivated not by political or military goals, but by the need to establish his identity through the arduous exercise of will-power: the ultimate senselessness of what he willed was, on this account, precisely the test of his resolve.

This iconoclastic, though deeply serious, reconstruction of Prussian history indicates how much Mann had to learn about political propaganda. Even more remote from the popular imagination are the *Reflections of a Nonpolitical Man (Betrachtungen eines Unpolitischen)*, a collection of essays written during the war and published in 1918, shortly after the collapse of the Wilhelmine order. As a quarry for ideological slogans, the *Reflections* look like 'Thoughts in Wartime' writ large and very, very long. Organic, vital German 'culture' is played off against the commercial, rationalistic, hedonistic 'civilisation' of 'the West'; the intuitive, 'musical' and apolitical German 'poet' is contrasted with the shallow, rhetorical, ideologising 'writer'; contractual democratic 'society' is compared unfavourably with status-based paternalistic 'community'; and there is much about a German mission to mediate between superficial 'Western' order and profound 'Asiatic' chaos.

Crude though these categories are, the *Reflections* set the intellectual agenda for much of Mann's later thinking about Germany, and consequently sketched out the groundwork for *Doctor Faustus*. The arguments remained important to Mann long after the initial source of their vehemence (a bitter public quarrel with his brother Heinrich, who was an outspoken critic of the German official ideology) had been put aside. Three abiding concerns stand out: a focus on Germany's self-consciously problematic relationship to modernity; an exploration of conflicts between the ethos of artistic creation and the demands of private and public morality; and, perhaps most importantly, a desire to take a stand on moral, cultural and political issues, uneasily combined with a deep suspicion of the blandishments of solidarity in either assent or dissent, a tension between didactic ambitions and radical individualism.

Despite later disavowals, the publication of *Reflections of a Nonpolitical Man* was in itself a political act, directed against the young Republic. The honorary doctorate bestowed on Mann by the University of Bonn in 1919 was partly in recognition of his role as early advocate of 'conservative revolution'. When he saw a soviet-style Republic being established and overthrown in Munich, his diaries recorded brief flirtations with Bolshevik sympathies, but more out of gleeful recognition of the affront to Entente liberalism than out of any sympathy for Lenin's political programme. As late as December 1921 he was reading the proofs for a second edition of the *Reflections* with satisfaction. Yet in 1922 Mann wrote (in August) and delivered (in October) an address 'Von deutscher Republik' (On the German Republic) which astonished both his supporters and opponents through its advocacy of democratic Republicanism and its disavowal of reactionary political programmes. His *plaidoyer* for the democratic constitution in this speech is at least as ironic and eccentric as his earlier contorted advocacy of Wilhelmine ideology. Novalis and Walt Whitman, two recent enthusiasms based on scant acquaintance, are pressed into service, to the exclusion of virtually every more relevant and plausible authority, and the new order is presented as an expression of Romantic vitalism, dating from the euphoria of August 1914 rather than from the grim lessons of 1918. This was the first of a series of occasions on which Thomas Mann offered his services as essayist and orator in defence of the Republic; as the 1920s advanced and the National Socialists were increasingly successful in channelling a spectrum of anti-democratic resentments and discontents into a formidable political force, Mann's public stance grew less eccentric and more supportive of the policies of the Social Democratic Party. This phase in his life is relived and reinterpreted in *The Magic Mountain*, a project already well under way by the outbreak of war, which was transformed both in scope and in overall tendency by the preoccupations worked through in the *Reflections* and the new political assessment of the 1920s. It appeared in the autumn of 1924, in Mann's fiftieth year. Mann then turned his attention to what was to develop into his longest fictional work, the novel tetralogy *Joseph and his Brothers*, the working-out of Mann's fascination with myth as a repository of stability in change.

Shortly after Hitler became Reich Chancellor in January 1933, Thomas Mann and his wife left Germany for a lecture tour in connection with the fiftieth anniversary of Richard Wagner's death. In various European cities, Mann delivered a characteristically ironic and ambivalent appreciation of Wagner, subsequently published as *Sufferings and Greatness of Richard Wagner* (IX, 363–426). A mixed bag of time-servers and zealots (including among the musical celebrities Knappertsbusch, Pfitzner and Richard Strauss) expressed organised public indignation at Mann's treatment of Wagner, which was starkly at odds with the expected tone and themes of 'national renewal'. He was advised by family and friends to delay his return, though he did not fully reconcile himself to staying abroad for good until 1936, when he was formally deprived of his German citizenship. Mann did not revisit Germany until 1949, and he never again settled there. There are some signs that he would have initially preferred what later, in the course of a sorry post-war controversy, became known as 'inner emigration'; though it is hard to see that as a genuine possibility in view of his temperament and his existing writings, including his literary exposure of the psychology of (Italian) fascism in *Mario and the Magician* (1929) and his scathing denunciations of fascism in policy and practice, especially his 'Deutsche Ansprache' (German Address) of 1930. He withdrew an initial promise to contribute to the exile journal *Die Sammlung* founded by his son Klaus so that the first volume of *Joseph and his Brothers* could go on sale in Germany, and he initially held aloof from other writers and intellectuals who, eagerly or by force of circumstances, had committed themselves to exile and public opposition to the Nazi regime. He found it hard to identify with them. For one thing, he did not share their general impoverishment, despite the confiscation of his property at home: he had shrewdly invested considerable sums abroad, and royalties from the sale of translations provided an additional income even when his works could no longer be sold in Germany. More important were the grounds for his exile. The bulk of his fellow exiles had been forced to flee for racial or political reasons: since he was neither Jewish nor a member of a left-wing organisation, Mann was reluctant to accept that his return was equally impossible. Three years elapsed before he expressed public opposition to the National Socialist regime, first in a letter of February 1936 to *Neue Zürcher Zeitung*, then, in the winter of 1936–37, in a pamphlet documenting his response to the withdrawal of German citizenship and the subsequent deprivation of his honorary degree by the University of Bonn. From this juncture, he became a prominent opponent of Hitler's government, though he always remained circumspect about joining or supporting émigré groups or activities.

The Anschluß of Austria in March 1938 came while Mann was on a lecture tour in North America: he decided it would be wiser to take up residence in the USA. Friends arranged for the issue of an immigrant's visa and a position as guest professor at Princeton (where Mann lived until moving to California early in 1941). He was a vocal and persistent critic of appeasement and isolationism, and served the Allied war effort by, among other things, recording a monthly commentary for transmission to Germany by the BBC. The remaining three volumes of the *Joseph* cycle were completed in the USA, as was the Goethe-novel *Lotte in Weimar*, begun in 1936 and finished in 1939. After the completion of *Joseph*, Mann wavered between two projects dating from some forty years earlier: the fictitious autobiography of a confidence trickster, some parts of which had been written between 1910 and 1913 and published in 1922; and the notion of rewriting the story of Faust in the form of the life of a syphilitic artist. This latter project, enormously complicated by the attempt to do justice to his subsequent experience, gained the upper hand and occupied him until early 1947. Only then did he turn to the completion of the first (and only) volume of the *Confessions of Felix Krull, Confidence Man*, his last work of any length.

An admirer of Franklin D. Roosevelt and of the vision of 'One World' that would unite the economic freedoms of capitalism with the social concerns of Marxism, Mann was profoundly disillusioned by post-war political developments. He viewed the rise of McCarthyism in the USA (where he had acquired citizenship in 1944) as a resurgence of fascism, leading him into a second exile. Unwilling to live in either of the two German states, he settled for the rest of his life near Zürich, where he died in August 1955.

Nietzsche's shadow

With *The Magic Mountain* and the works that followed, Mann gained a reputation as a highly intellectual writer. There is an incontestable sense in which he is precisely that: his novels in general, and many of their principal characters in particular, show a voluble concern with issues of a high order of generality. The life of the mind, and above all the impact of ideas upon the way people experience themselves and their place in the world, is one of his chief thematic preoccupations. However, Mann himself was hardly an intellectual, and certainly not a philosopher, as many of his less critical admirers, past and present, like to believe. He was an imaginative writer with an unusual gift for spotting the broad implications of certain leading ideas and exploring their impact on the lives of invented characters. He did not extend or refine the ideas he took up in his various fictions; the closest he came to making a genuine intellectual, as distinct from creative, contribution to contemporary culture was in the way he explored what happens when ideas impinge upon the passions, aspirations and inhibitions of representative citizens of modern Europe.

For all the panoply of names likely to turn up in the index of a book surveying Mann's work, from Abraham a Santa Clara through to Zoroaster, passing on the way Einstein, Freud, Jung, Luther, Kant, Kierkegaard, Hegel, Marx, and many others, there is really only one thinker with whom he engaged on anything more than an occasional, instrumental, and often second- or third-hand level for the limited span of a particular project: Friedrich Nietzsche (1844–1900). Mann belonged to the generation of fin-de-siècle writers for whom Nietzsche's thought became the chief tool both for understanding their own psychology as authors, and for exploring the workings of their culture, suggesting both the aims and the techniques for their artistic careers. Mann's indebtedness to Nietzsche encompasses both the content and the means of his fiction through all its phases, and it colours his reception and use of every other intellectual – and artistic – influence on his work.

As far as the subject-matter of Mann's fiction is concerned, the impact of Nietzsche is most plainly visible in the predominant theme of disablement through excessive consciousness. Consciousness, as it has developed in Western European culture, was seen by Nietzsche as subversive of vitality in two main ways. First, awareness and analysis were allegedly fostered at the expense of spontaneity and vital exuberance: thinking had replaced action. Secondly, modern intellectuals were obsessed with amassing all available knowledge about the self and the world, heedless of the consequences for a sense of purpose or identity: excessive awareness had undermined the self-respect and lamed the healthy self-assertion of individuals and of cultures. The undermining of vitality by insight, the struggle to sustain 'life-enhancing' illusions by sheer will-power: these are the raw materials from which the psychology of nearly all Mann's characters is built, and the efforts of such characters to survive in an inhospitable world is the stuff of most of his plots.

Less obvious, but in the end more important for Mann's artistic development, is the influence which Nietzsche had on Mann's literary techniques. Mann's perspectivism is his response to Nietzsche's understanding of the way that truthfulness might still be pursued in the inexorable absence of truth. For the imperative to truthfulness persists in Nietzsche, despite his conviction that all substantial 'truths', great and small, are delusions. There can be for him no truth, because there is no being, only endless flux, precariously fixed and therefore inevitably falsified by the provisional constructions of thought and language. 'There are no *eternal facts*, any more than there are any absolute truths. That is why from now on we need historical philosophising and along with it the virtue of modesty', he wrote in *Human, All Too Human* (Schlechta I, 448). 'Historical philosophising' involves, among other things, a comprehensive reciprocal relativisation of all viewpoints and opinions; and it requires 'modesty' because the 'historical' thinker, tracing the genesis through time of alleged 'eternal facts', must resist the temptation to believe he possesses superior 'facts' (as distinct from a possibly more appropriate method). The literary correlative of this approach is a narrative technique that, in the interests of truthfulness, embeds all perceptions and judgements in the rendered experience of a plurality of characters, none of whose individual perspectives is given final validity. Mann's use of parody is also a Nietzschean trait. Parody as Mann practises it, especially in *Doctor Faustus*, is a pre-eminently 'historical' way of relativising values and beliefs by consciously 'citing' them as phenomena with a cultural history and so foregrounding their appeal to our interest rather than their claims to validity. It could be argued that the development of Mann's narrative approach after *Buddenbrooks* shows an increasingly elaborate pursuit of narrative truthfulness along lines suggested by Nietzsche's views, with the culmination in *Doctor Faustus*, where perspectivism and parody are carried to an extreme degree.

In a celebrated passage in the *Reflections* (XII, 79), Mann writes of a 'constellation of three stars' in his intellectual firmament: Nietzsche, Schopenhauer and Wagner. But every reference he makes, discursive or creative, to the last two is unmistakeably stamped by the imprint of the first. In particular, Mann sees Wagner as Nietzsche came to view him after he had turned against his former idol, namely as an insidious purveyor of Schopenhauer's erotically charged pessimism. In most of Mann's works, music figures as a subverter of all order, social and moral, a sensuously alluring embodiment of the blandishments of decay and death. The grip of this view of music over his imagination can be seen most clearly in the episode in *The Magic Mountain* where Hans Castorp's enthralment to death is figured and analysed through a description of his response to five pieces of music. Wagner is conspicuously absent by name (indeed, the composers concerned – Debussy, Gounod, Bizet, Verdi and Schubert – seem a deliberately un-Wagnerian bunch), but the understanding of the significance and effects of their music is all of a piece with the debilitating intoxication through which Wagnerian chromaticism gnawed away at young Hanno Buddenbrook's will to live. So Mann's understanding of the power and philosophical significance of music, which shaped his decision to make his representative German artist a composer, was substantially derived from Nietzsche; only when the novel was under way did Mann encounter, via Adorno, another view of music which had a significant effect on the way the work in progress developed.

Mann's original notion of writing a version of Faust in the guise of a syphilitic artist, first noted down around 1905 (Mann later mistakenly assigned the jotting to 1901, misled by the date on the cover of his notebook) also bears the unmistakeable stamp of Nietzsche. Apart from the parallel to the assumed syphilitic nature of Nietzsche's illness, the motif of creative sterility overcome by desperate means in the absence of natural vitality obviously draws on a facet of Nietzsche's cultural analysis, while the idea of reducing artistic inspiration, with the quasi-divine aura it had been lent by Romanticism, to the effects of a highly disreputable disease is very much in the fashion of what Nietzsche called his 'evil eye', his penchant for gleefully uncovering degraded and degrading origins for things generally treated with piety. Mann's decision to make his Faust a composer, which was not (necessarily) part of the earliest plan, must also have been shaped by the understanding of music which Mann derived from Nietzsche, though the fact that the first real-life 'syphilitic artist' whose biography he investigated at any length was Hugo Wolf doubtless also played a part. And the narrative structure of the work, the way the life is 'told by a friend', as the subtitle says, also owes a great deal to Nietzsche, both because it is an eminently perspectivist device, and because it reflects the way Nietzsche himself attracted the solicitous but in the end ineffectual friendship of people whose temperament and outlook were very different from his own.

This leads to the most obvious and pervasive sense in which Mann's Faust is a Nietzschean figure, the fact that the broad plan and many of the details of Leverkühn's biography are closely modelled on Nietzsche's own life. Adrian Leverkühn thinks of himself as Faust, Mann invites us to think of him as Faust and Nietzsche combined. It is an association which one is surprised, with hindsight, that Nietzsche did not make himself. It was certainly not modesty that prevented him.

More likely it was the place that Faust had come to occupy in nineteenth-century German ideology that stopped Nietzsche from making the link that to Thomas Mann seemed so plausible. Before Mann's novel, Faust was a figure heavily overlaid with Wilhelmine accretions: in writing a *Faust* for the mid twentieth century he was also recovering the import and the ethos of the original literary *Faust*, and restating its claim to a place of its own in German literary and intellectual history.

Faust in history

The first *Faust* was the creation of an anonymous author who brought together various tales about magicians then circulating in Germany, assigned them all to one Johann Faust (who has a shadowy historical existence) and composed for this loose assembly of anecdotes a beginning and an end, telling how Faust came to acquire his powers through a pact with the devil, and how in fulfilment of that pact he was finally dragged off to Hell. He also contributed an episode in which Faust, after seventeen years of his twenty-four-year pact, is brought close to repentance by a pious neighbour, only to draw back and recommit himself even more ferociously to the devil's cause. The result was published in Frankfurt in 1587, becoming known, after the publisher's name, as the Spies *Faustbuch*. The portions contributed by the unknown author are vehemently religious and didactic. He execrates all aspirations to learn things not conveyed in the Bible, for it is primarily the appetite for such knowledge that drives Faust to his satanic pact. This castigation of human curiosity must be understood in the context of the *Faustbuch*'s origins in the last quarter of the sixteenth century, an age that had seen the Voyages of Discovery, the Renaissance revival of classical scholarship and the first stirrings of what would become the new science of Nature. The thirst for knowledge which drives Faust away from respectable scholarship into the arms of the devil also makes him embody the great historical movement of his day towards the expansion of knowledge by secular enquiry, a movement which the author is both acknowledging and attempting to condemn as fundamentally evil.

He would doubtless have been dismayed to know that precisely that secular culture whose beginnings he tried to anathematise would come to see his Faust as the archetype of a cultural hero, a champion of individualism emancipating itself from ecclesiastical tutelage.

After the publication of the 1587 chapbook, the Faust tradition bifurcated. One strand remained in the German-speaking countries, as the *Faustbuch* was pirated, expanded, expurgated and glossed by a variety of editors, remaining more or less constantly in print down the centuries. The other strand crossed to England, where Christopher Marlowe saw the dramatic potential of the story and made it the basis of his play *The Tragicall History of the Life and Death of Doctor Faustus* (date uncertain: between 1588 and 1593). Next, in a strange development, Marlowe's *Faustus* found its way back to Germany, not in the original or in anything like a faithful translation, but through heavily adapted and simplified versions performed by itinerant theatre companies, which in turn provided a model for slapstick puppet plays that were a common fairground attraction in seventeenth- and eighteenth-century Germany. It was in this form that the material fired Goethe's dramatic imagination: he did not encounter Marlowe's *Doctor Faustus* until long after completing Part I of his *Faust* tragedy in 1801 (Thomas Mann, incidentally, does not seem to have known Marlowe's play at all).

The essential thematic bond between Goethe's play and the Faustbuch is that both are concerned with questions about values and conduct raised by the culture that germinated in the Renaissance and first flowered in the Enlightenment. But where the *Faustbuch* author was probably ignorant of the historical implications of his theme, Goethe constructed his play, and in particular Part I, as a tragedy of modernity. His Faust, though ostensibly a disillusioned scholar like his sixteenth-century predecessor, is not interested either in mere information about the universe or in material wealth: he wants to achieve a direct apprehension, sensuous and intellectual at the same time, of the principle of dynamism in cohesion which he believes is at the very core of the universe. He enlists demonic assistance to expand the boundaries of his self to encompass the whole gamut of possible human experience. In this aspiration, he is following the disaffection of the *Sturm und Drang* writers of the 1770s with rational enquiry and abstract knowledge, striving to become a 'genius' in the sense of someone possessing a uniquely strong appetite and high capacity for feeling, especially feeling which intuits the presence of cosmic forces transcending reason and draws sustenance from them. It was consequently Goethe who first clearly aligned Faust with the personality and aims of the creative artist. In his quest for breadth and intensity of experience, Faust becomes fascinated by Gretchen, whom with diabolical aid he seduces and abandons. Initially secure within the old order sanctioned by religion and social hierarchy, Gretchen comes to grief through the eruption into her life of a modern, insatiably searching and uncompromisingly secular individualist. Goethe's work is incomparably more subtle in its moral vision as well as in its artistry than anything we find in the *Faustbuch*. Nevertheless, the issues with which it engages, at a much higher artistic level and from a different historical situation, are identifiably continuous with some of the *Faustbuch* author's concerns.

The moral (and dramatic) complexity of Goethe's *Faust* was lost on most of his contemporaries and successors in the nineteenth and early twentieth centuries. A crude stereotype of Faust as an exemplar of self-assertion in the cause of 'higher' humanity led to the coining of the concept of 'das Faustische' as an (a)moral ideal for which Goethe's authority was incongruously assumed. Oswald Spengler, in his influential *The Decline of the West* (1918–22), designated his picture of the present and final age of Western culture, one of soulless technology, mindless regimentation and unscrupulous imperialist expansion, as 'Faustian', in the confident expectation that his readers would find it all a Good Thing. And of course, there was no shortage of literary scholars in the Germany of the 1930s eager to demonstrate the 'Faustian' virtues of the Führer and his Movement. Mann needed to scrape off these ideological encrustations before the undiminished core of significance in the Faust tradition could be made visible once again.

Though judgements that artists 'had' to choose one subject rather than another should always be viewed with suspicion, it is tempting to say that Thomas Mann 'had', by virtue of his public career and personal creative concerns, to write his version of the Faust story when he did. Some sort of public reckoning with Germany's past and present could hardly be avoided by a writer with Mann's career behind him. And the Faust material, with its strong links both to the origins of modern Europe in the Reformation and Renaissance and to the burgeoning of German intellectual and literary culture in the eighteenth century, seems an obvious choice for a writer who believed that the phenomenon of fascism was a response to the breakdown of the cultural order whose beginnings and highest achievements were signalled respectively by the *Faustbuch* and Goethe's Faust. Last but not least, there was the opportunity to consummate the half-serious, half-playful self-identification with Goethe in which Mann indulged himself during the latter half of his life. Goethe had worked on his *Faust* for the greater part of his creative existence and treated Part II as his spiritual testament. Mann felt that his days were numbered (he begins *Doctor Faustus. The Genesis of a Novel*, his otherwise not particularly revealing account of the origins of the work, with the remark that he had expected to die in 1945). He saw the chance to make his putatively last work the fulfilment of an idea he had first jotted down as a young man, into which he could build his personal history, the spiritual biography of his philosophical mentor, and the fate of his nation. For all the pitfalls, the project was too alluring to resist.

Chapter 2

An artist's life

The magic square

As in so many of Thomas Mann's fictions, an apparently simple narrative surface hides virtually inexhaustible layers of complexity. Serenus Zeitblom, a schoolmaster in his sixties living in provincial Bavaria, who gave up his job after Hitler's seizure of power, writes the biography of Adrian Leverkühn, a composer known to him since childhood who has died two years previously after a decade of insanity. What we read is not so much a finished biography as a draft incorporating Zeitblom's many and various reflections about the circumstances and ostensible defects of his writing. Indeed, for all his hyper-literary style, Zeitblom seems to imagine himself addressing a potentially fractious audience, rather than writing for a future readership: one does not, after all, ask such a readership's permission to start a rambling sentence again, as Zeitblom does in his very first paragraph (p. 9, LP 1), the first of a series of such apologetic self-corrections. Zeitblom begins writing in May 1943, after Stalingrad and German reverses in North Africa have made it clear that the tide of war has turned against Hitler: he brings his story to an end shortly after the German capitulation two years later, when most of Germany's cities are in ruins. (The actual composition of the novel took Thomas Mann rather longer: his real starting date coincided with the fictional one, but the novel was not completed until January 1947.) The story Zeitblom tells starts with Leverkühn's birth in 1875 and finishes with his mental collapse in 1930, with a brief glimpse of the decade of insanity before his death in 1940. The span of the novel's thematic concerns, however, covers several centuries of European culture.

Leverkühn deliberately lives his life as a series of references to the Faust story as told in the chapbook of 1587. And Zeitblom, as he ponders the story of his friend and the history of his nation as it works itself out around him, comes to sense analogies between the destiny of his friend and the broader course of events, to such an extent that, when plagued by tremors of his writing hand, or bouts of psycho-somatic illness, he is unsure whether past or present happenings are the cause. So Zeitblom is, under one aspect, a device for elaborating on the significance of Adrian Leverkühn's life. But he is also himself a representatively German character. It is not just Leverkühn's biography, but the interrelation of Zeitblom's and Leverkühn's lives, which creates the complex fictitious construct we are offered as Mann's response to German history. The need to interpret Leverkühn and Zeitblom together in their interacting contributions to this construct is doubtless what Thomas Mann had chiefly in mind when he wrote of his two figures concealing 'the secret of their identity' (XI, 204). It is a twofold secret, encompassing both the claim that they embody two sides of the same issue, the problematic history of modern Germany, and the sense that each one, taken alone, is merely a partial projection of Mann's own self-understanding. The two of them together are, in one sense, Germany; and in another sense, they are Thomas Mann as he sees himself in retrospect. This fiction is as close as Mann ever came to a comprehensive autobiography.

It should be plain already that the issues of parallelism and representativeness in this novel are complicated enough to describe, let alone interpret. The most deeply embedded parallel is that between Leverkühn and the Faust of the *Faustbuch*, since it is established by Leverkühn himself, who quite consciously aligns significant events in his life with the *Faustbuch* paradigm. The broadening of the parallel Leverkühn-Faust to encompass the span of modern German history is undertaken, in the first instance, by Zeitblom. But a further set of parallels, the result of what Mann called his 'montage technique' (XI, 165), is invisible to characters within the fiction. Mann incorporated numerous motifs, from a vast range of fictional, historical, and personal-domestic sources into Leverkühn's life-story, mingling them virtually undetectably with his own inventions. The most significant are the borrowings from

Nietzsche's life, so detailed and extensive that Mann declared Nietzsche could not exist within the domain of the fiction other than in the guise of Leverkühn (XI, 165). We have here a hierarchy of interacting parallels: at the base Leverkühn's life; then Zeitblom's understanding of its significance; and then an overarching third level in the network of allusions generated by our perception of Zeitblom and Leverkühn as interdependent fictional constructs subordinate to an immensely complex grand design. Leverkühn's self-identification with the Faust figure is reflected upon and relativised both by his fictitious biographer and by the all-disposing author of the novel as a 'magic square' which can and must be read in several directions at once.

A normal childhood?

From the earliest stages of Zeitblom's account, it is plain he believes his friend lived out a particular 'destiny' whose seeds lay in his distinctive personality, though it required a highly specific cultural-historical juncture for its unfolding and fulfilment. The most obvious mark that Adrian Leverkühn is so singled out is his exceptional solitude, associated with two interrelated psychological traits, emotional coldness and pride, which find expression in a particular kind of sardonic laughter, his uniform response from an early age to a wide spectrum of experiences. Given Mann's marked predilection for attaching great weight to conflicting parental influences as a source of his heroes' identity problems, we understandably look to Leverkühn's parentage and upbringing for some clue to his psychological make-up. Commonly, his heroes have to establish their identity through an inner struggle upon lines broadly determined by contrasting parental temperaments and attitudes, which work both through an inherited 'mixed' temperament in the child and through tensions in the child's relationship with the mother on the one hand and the father on the other. Beyond this, as his central characters approach maturity, their identity is often shaped through conflict between child and home in the two spheres with which the modern consolidation of male personality is generally located: choice of career and selection of a marriage partner.

At first sight, the most striking thing about Johann and Elsbeth Leverkühn is their normality compared to parents in other works by Mann. A tendency to migraine (though, we are assured, 'only to a slight degree ... with virtually no effect on his working life') (p. 21, LP 10) and slightly eccentric tastes in reading material are the only signs of anything like oddity in Johann Leverkühn, the father; and to anyone familiar with the more or less exotic maternal figures elsewhere in Mann, the account of the mother's provenance reads like parody by understatement. Where Tonio Kröger's father fetched his bride 'from way down on the map', Elsbeth Leverkühn comes from all of fifty kilometres away, though admittedly in a southerly direction, and there is certainly nothing hot-blooded about her. It might seem that Mann had spared Leverkühn any childhood traumas stemming from heredity or family environment, and restricted his penchant for depicting domestic conflict to the Munich milieu of the later parts of the novel, where the Rodde family and their associates place the austere hero and his pedantic biographer against a background of pervasive cultural and moral decadence.

Yet there is, after all, something strange about Leverkühn's relationship to his childhood surroundings, brought out by his choosing to spend eighteen years, most of his creative life, at Pfeiffering in Bavaria, cut off from his real family and yet in an ambience bearing an uncanny resemblance to his home in Saxony. Zeitblom remarks that '[the choice of such a dwelling-place] was all the more puzzling in Leverkühn's case, seeing that I had never observed his relationship to his parental home to be especially intense or emotional, and that he had left it behind him, quite early in his life, with no signs of pain' (p. 40, LP 24). Zeitblom respects this attitude to such an extent that he leaves Elsbeth Leverkühn in ignorance of her son's breakdown until it is plain that his insanity is complete and incurable, and that his Bavarian surrogate 'mother', Frau Schweigestill, cannot be expected to cope with it. Only then, when the Leverkühn's adult self has been destroyed by mental illness, is he reunited with his natural mother. 'He was not to return to her,' Zeitblom had remarked, speaking of Leverkühn's farewell to his mother, some twenty years earlier, ' – and he never wanted to. She came to him' (p. 259, LP 197).

All this raises a suspicion that the childhood may be, after all, in some way 'deprived', though in a subtler sense than Mann usually portrays, that something in Leverkühn's early life makes a significant contribution to the identity crisis which he later resorts to such drastic means to resolve. Leverkühn, as we shall see, is described as a personality with a void where we should expect an emotional centre. But he is gripped from his adolescence by a 'passion' for music which fills out this void and around which he builds his life. His mother has no such dramatic emptiness, but there is at least a partial void in her personality, an aspect of herself which she suppresses; and this suppression has to do with music, the sole abiding object of her son's passion:

> The most beautiful thing about her [Zeitblom tells us] was her voice, a warm mezzo-soprano in pitch ... [Its] charm came from an inner musicality, which otherwise remained latent, since Elsbeth took no interest in music, refused as it were to admit to it ... She never really let herself get involved with proper singing, though I would be willing to bet that there was excellent potential to be developed there.
>
> (pp. 33–4, LP 20)

Describing her return as an old woman into her son's life, Zeitblom once again refers to her voice, 'still as melodious as ever, which her whole life long she had forbidden to sing' (p. 673, LP 52). And what is implied by this self-imposed 'prohibition', this 'refusal to admit to' or 'let herself get involved with' music, is hinted at when Zeitblom tells us how as boys, he and Adrian were taught to sing folk-songs by the earthy dairy-maid, 'an activity from which Elsbeth Leverkühn, with her beautiful voice, abstained out of a sort of chastity' (p. 41, LP 25). To complete the network of associations between singing and sexuality, we find Leverkühn himself talking of the supreme sensuousness of the singing voice: 'Abstract it may well be, the human voice – the abstract human being, if you like. But it's a kind of abstraction rather like the abstraction of the naked body — it's virtually a sexual organ' (p. 95, LP 67).

Few things are more tedious, or more irrelevant to literary understanding, than grinding fictional infancies through a psychoanalytic mill. But there does seem here to be a tissue of suggestions that Leverkühn's sexual aloofness, his 'armour of purity and chastity' (p. 197, LP 149), linked as it is to his 'coldness' and his solitude, has some connection with his mother's 'abstention' from sensuality in a domain which will come to mean so much to her son. And if we pursue the notion, present in one form or another from purest Freudian orthodoxy through to the most radical French revisionism, that in modern European cultures the male infant learns desire from and for the mother and law from and through the father, we can see Johann Leverkühn's eccentric interests as another part of a pattern of divergence from the 'normal' acquisition of selfhood. Transgression and its interdiction by 'Le "Non" du Père' are possible only where there are firm boundaries, and Adrian's father takes special delight in blurring borders, pointing out to his son instances where categories dissolve into one another. His illustrated books of flora and fauna and his scientific experiments lead him to 'mystical' reflections on 'the unity of inanimate and so-called inanimate nature' (p. 29, LP 16) and on instances where the distinctions of conventional science are undercut by drops of liquid that 'digest' other drops, by crystal 'plants' that 'grow' in the direction of sunlight (p. 29, LP 17), and other phenomena which Zeitblom finds 'spooky' (p. 32, LP 18) and threatening because they undermine that decisive articulation of experience which is the precondition of stable meaning.

So if the mother protects herself and vainly tries to protect her child against the allurements of desire, the father, far from enforcing discipline and law, actually subverts paternal rigour and clarity. Adrian Leverkühn's childhood is deficient in the primary influences by which the male self is formed in the modern nuclear family. Neither initiated into the realm of desire by his mother nor confronted with the clarity of law by his father, he achieves no accommodation between desire and law in a 'normally' socialised self. Instead, at the core of his personality is a gaping absence, a solitude which Zeitblom compares to 'an abyss, into which feelings directed towards him disappeared soundlessly and without trace', and 'all around him is *coldness*' (p. 13, LP 4). Or again, in vocabulary which introduces one dimension of the novel's discourse of salvation and damnation to which we shall have to return at greater length, 'characters like Adrian do not have much soul', with 'soul' being glossed as 'an intermediate, mediating organ, deeply steeped in poetry, in which mind and instincts interpenetrate each other and come to a certain illusory accommodation'. In his psychic economy, 'intellect and naked drives confront one another in the most direct way conceivable' (p. 197, LP 149). The whole of the middle ground, the domain of 'soul', of relatively stable selfhood which is constructed when desire and order intertwine in dynamic tension, seems to be missing; and its lack does not just prevent Leverkühn from relating to other, more conventionally structured selves; it also makes him incapable of dealing in the spiritual and emotional currency in which the interchange among such selves is conducted and of sharing in the culture of romantic individualism within which that currency circulates. As the height of his life's creative achievement, and with the help of forces the novel insists on calling diabolical, Leverkühn coins his own currency to express the essence of his solitude, a musical idiom which draws both its dynamics and its structure from the direct confrontation of raw impersonal instinct and mercilessly systematic abstraction, the inspiration he has bought by a 'demonic pact' and the formal idiom he has forged by unrelievedly solitary efforts of intellect and will. But to do that he has first to recognise his destiny as musician, and, having recognised it, 'admit to' its reality, and face up to its cost.

A passionate interest

Leverkühn's discovery of his vocation, one principal component in the establishment of his adult identity, follows lines already laid down by his childhood; and that vocation will subsume in his eyes the other sphere of life that generally ratifies the identity of the fully socialised individual: his marriage partner. In his own phrase he will marry his profession — music itself as recreated by his demonic genius (p. 175, LP 131).

In his emotional emptiness, Leverkühn engages with the world only through his analytical intelligence, unchecked by any personal or historical pieties. 'Do you think love is the most powerful of passions?' he sceptically asks Zeitblom, and adds that he knows of a passion stronger still: 'interest' (p. 95, LP 67), where the German term 'Interesse' needs glossing in English as intellectual fascination. That remark dates from Adrian's late adolescence, when he is still searching in vain for an object of intellectual curiosity which can offer sufficient resistance to his mind to win his respect and to stave off the boredom, 'the coldest thing in the world', with which most things leave him once he has swiftly 'seen through' how they work. What people around him find fascinating, moving or even awe-inspiring, from his father's illustrations of the mimicry of exotic insects through to the delight which Zeitblom, the classical scholar, takes in the Mediterranean landscape during his visit to Italy, engage Leverkühn's attention only for as long as it takes to see how they operate. Then after brief amusement, producing his characteristic laughter 'when others have tears in their eyes', boredom returns. Only one school subject strikes him, if not quite as 'interesting' in his rigorous sense, at least as 'entertaining': mathematics. What gives mathematics its power to occupy his intelligence for longer than other subjects is its formal nature, which can engage his intellect when disciplines with a finite and consequently exhaustible substance prove wanting and earn only his 'ironic disdain'. Mathematics, Zeitblom explains,

remains in lofty heights of pure abstraction ... [and] occupies a peculiar intermediate position between humanistic and scientific disciplines ... [Leverkühn] felt this position was superior, dominant, universal, or, as he expressed it, 'the real thing'. It gladdened my heart to hear him call something 'the real thing', it was an anchor, a foothold, one no longer asked oneself wholly in vain what 'really counted' for him.

This conversation issues into one of the 'revelations' with which the young Leverkühn periodically surprises his friend, and which is extremely significant for the thematic architecture of the novel.

'You're an oaf', he said to me, 'not to like [mathematics]. After all, contemplating orderly relationships is the best thing there is. Order is everything. Romans thirteen: "There is no order but from God." ' He blushed, and I stared at him wide-eyed. It emerged that he was religious. (p. 64, LP 43–4)

How far Adrian Leverkühn, with his inaccurate quotations from scripture, can be described as 'religious' in any sense that stands up outside the novel's network of analogical references is another question to which we shall have to return. What counts in this passage as far as the establishment of Leverkühn's identity is concerned is his fascination with a clarity of order which his father's blurring of boundaries had undercut, and his discovery of such order at the highest level of abstraction. Zeitblom now tells us that this particular revelation had in fact been preceded by another, which he only now relates: he had 'caught' his fourteen-year-old friend 'secretly exploring' harmonic relationships on an old harmonium (p. 65, LP 44). With furtive excitement, he has worked out for himself the system of key-relationships on the tempered keyboard, and is particularly fascinated by the tuning that makes enharmonic modulations possible.

He sounded a chord, all black notes, F sharp, A sharp, C sharp, added an E and so unmasked the chord, which had looked like F sharp major, as belonging to B major, namely its dominant. 'A combination of notes like that', he said, 'isn't in itself in any key. It's all a matter of relationships, and the relationships form a circle ... Relationship is everything [this is, of course, a deliberate echo of his 'order is everything' apropos mathematics]. And if you want a better name for it, then its proper name is 'ambiguity' ... 'Do you know what I think?' he asked. 'Music is ambiguity as system' ... He had flushed cheeks, which never happened with schoolwork, not even with algebra. (pp. 65–6, LP 45)

So in music Leverkühn has found a domain that offers the endless allurements of ambiguity (here: the dissolution of distinctions between one key and another) in combination with the stability of a lucid and wholly intelligible system of laws. It is a set of rule-governed relationships which generates elaborate ambiguities out of itself, so that those ambiguities exist in dynamic interchange with the order which is their precondition. Music thus understood brings together the clarity of law and the excitements of transgression into a fusion which is an image of that integrated self which Leverkühn lacks.

Not only music as system, but music as sensory phenomenon partakes for Leverkühn of the same 'interesting' combination of extremes. This is prefigured in his childhood introduction to music by Hanne, the dairy-maid with wobbly bosom and a strong animal smell (p. 41, LP 25) who shows her enjoyment of imitative counterpoint (Zeitblom assures us that the canons she teaches the children represent 'a relatively high stage of musical development' (p. 43, LP 27)) by a grin that resembles a dog catching sight of its dinner (p. 42, LP 26). As an adolescent, Leverkühn will remark how the Dutch polyphonists

made music perform the most elaborate tricks to the glory of God, highly unsensuous and worked out purely mathematically. But then they had people *sing* these penitential exercises, delivering them up to the musical sound of human breath, which has more animal warmth in it than any other instrument you can think of ... The rigour of this music, what you might call the moral discipline of its form, has to provide a justification for its intoxicatingly sensuous sound.

(p. 95, LP 67)

Music as orderly system generating endless ambiguities, and music as the disciplined embodiment of the highest degree of tension between the sensuous and the intellectual, these are the things that sow in Leverkühn the seeds of what Zeitblom sees with sombre premonition as a lifelong passion which he will prefer to all human involvements.

But passionate fascination is not the same as a sense of vocation, which requires a vision of how a private preoccupation can relate to the wider world of human activity. Leverkühn is provided with just such a vision by the organist Kretzschmar, both through his public lectures to a sparse and bemused audience in Zeitblom's home town of Kaisersaschern, where

Leverkühn is attending grammar school, and during the piano lessons which Leverkühn begins at his uncle's suggestion, after his experimentation with harmony is overheard. In these lessons a good half of the time goes on conversations about philosophy and literature (p. 99, LP 70), for Kretzschmar is, like Settembrini and Naphta in *The Magic Mountain*, a 'discursive character' and an extraordinarily digressive one as well.

Shooting off at a tangent and drawing parallels, he got further and further away from his initial point ... because he was passionately fond of making comparisons, revealing connections, demonstrating influences, laying bare the complex intertwining of cultural links.
(p. 103, LP 75)

Kretzschmar's encyclopaedic vision sets the development of music in a much broader historical-cultural process, and conveys, through his depiction of the compositional struggles of the late Beethoven in particular, the idea that this process is carried out in and through the crises of particular individuals, whose problems are accordingly neither merely personal nor technical, but components in a broad cultural movement. He portrays strenuous isolation as the distinctively modern mode of musical creative existence, depicting Beethoven's battle with the fugal textures of the *Missa Solemnis* as a parallel to Christ's agony in the garden, so introducing into the novel the Gethsemane motif which Zeitblom will detect and expand upon in Leverkühn's last work. Kretzschmar also, most crucially for Leverkühn's discovery of his own path in life, talks of future developments which will overcome this phase of art as solitary redemptive labour, so inspiring in Leverkühn the idea that 'the secularisation of art ... the separation of art from the liturgical whole, its liberation ... into an autonomous cultural domain, had burdened it with an absolute gravity, a solemn cult of suffering ... that need not be its abiding destiny' and the notion that art is destined to return 'to a more modest, happier [role] in the service of a higher community which need not necessarily be, as it was in the past, the church'(p. 82, LP 57).

This is heady stuff. Kretzschmar is propounding not simply the unremarkable belief that art has a history which is bound up in wider patterns of change, but the metaphysical claim that there is a purpose (as well as, less contentiously, a pattern) in those changes, that this purpose 'uses' individuals to fulfil itself, and that such individuals can realise their destiny by working through the contradictions within their own experience and thus carry the process forward. This is very different from the modernist view of the isolated artist à la Rilke, James Joyce or Proust, who finds a private salvation by detaching himself from contingency and history, holding otherwise fragmentary and centrifugal moments of private experience together through the power of imagination, and fusing these fragments of meaning together into a highly individual work of art which makes them accessible to those gifted with an appropriate sensibility. On the contrary, informing Kretzschmar's account of the distinctive isolation of the modern artist is the notion that the apparent senselessness of history is just a spur to the artist's rediscovery of pattern, which can somehow be part of the reconstruction of a society and history once more pervaded with meaning, bringing the artist's human isolation to an end. When, some three years later, Kretzschmar marshals the arguments that successfully persuade Leverkühn to dedicate himself to composition, the Hegelian ancestry of his ideas is unmistakeable:

Art progresses, [he argues] ... and it does so by means of the individual personality, the product and tool of the age, in which objective and subjective motives are combined to the point of indistinguishability, the one taking on the guise of the other. The vital need of art for revolutionary progress and the emergence of something new depends on the vehicle of an intense subjective sense of the exhaustion ... of current techniques, and it makes use of something apparently un-dynamic, of individual fatigue and intellectual boredom ... art's will to live and progress takes on the mask of these bland personal characteristics in order to manifest, to objectify, to fulfil itself.

(p. 180, LP 136)

This ascription of purposes to art is not a metaphorical device but a metaphysical assertion. Kretzschmar is inviting his pupil to see himself as akin to one of Hegel's world-historical personalities, suggesting that precisely the obstacles Leverkühn foresees to his becoming a composer are part of the 'cunning of reason' by which 'art', a handmaid of history itself, is summoning him to fulfil 'its' needs, with his inhibitions being so many (dialectical) signs of his vocation to move music forward.

Kretzschmar's theory makes precisely Leverkühn's anxieties about whether composition is his true vocation into decisive evidence for his calling. These doubts are profound and comprehensive, covering both his individual personality and the situation of art in the modern world as Kretzschmar has taught him to understand it. The doubts stemming from his personal make-up have to do with the oddity of someone whose chief emotional characteristic is 'coldness' becoming involved in an essentially expressive art. 'I fear, my friend and teacher,' he responds to one of Kretzschmar's efforts to persuade him to embrace composition, 'that I'm a bad sort, for I lack warmth' (p. 174, LP 131). Then there is the difficulty which he anticipates that his penetrating intellect will create when it comes to accepting and extending the received technical devices of music.

I'm afraid to take my vows to art ... because I have to admit that I lack the robust naivety that is ... part of being an artist. Instead I've been given an intelligence that quickly becomes satiated, and that ... is the reason for my reluctance and my anxiety ... Young as I am, I know my way around art enough to realise ... that there is much more to it than just ... convention, tradition, what one learns from others, the 'knack' of doing things; but all the same, there's always a great deal of that kind of thing bound up with art, and I can see it coming... that I'll grow unhappy with the worn-out, familiar material, which is the underlying skeleton ... even of works of genius, with all the aspects of art that are common property, cultural tradition, with the accepted ways of achieving beauty − I can see myself becoming embarrassed by it, see it tiring me out, giving me a headache, and all too soon, at that. (p. 178, LP 133−4)

'Headaches' of the kind he here anticipates did not come, as he has earlier explained, 'from over-exertion, but from tedium, from chilling boredom', from the grim awareness that his mind has exhausted a topic and it has lost all 'interest' for him. The most important of Adrian Leverkühn's grounds for 'abstinence'

(p. 178, LP 133) from music, however, extends these personal reservations into a large-scale cultural critique. And it is at this point, where the notion of the 'work' of art comes under scrutiny, that the long-standing influence of Nietzsche was joined by ideas which Mann acquired from Adorno.

The making of a modernist

Theodor Wiesengrund Adorno (1903–69), philosopher, sociologist, musicologist, literary critic and aesthetic theoretician, had written a doctoral thesis on Husserl's phenomenology in Frankfurt, studied composition under Alban Berg in Vienna, and qualified as a university teacher with a study of Kierkegaard strongly influenced by the aesthetic and religious ideas of Walter Benjamin. Associated with the 'Institute for Social Research' (the origin of the 'Frankfurt School') around Max Horkheimer, Adorno emigrated to the USA, where Horkheimer had found him work at Princeton. In 1941, he followed Horkheimer to Los Angeles and began work with him on what was eventually to be published in 1947 as *Dialektik der Aufklärung* (Dialectic of Enlightenment), a primary text of the Frankfurt School and its Critical Theory. He also pursued his own musicological and aesthetic research, the results of which appeared, again in 1947 in his *Philosophie der neuen Musik* (Philosophy of Modern Music). Adorno lent Mann the manuscript of the first part of this work, dealing chiefly with Schoenberg, in the summer of 1943. From this point onwards, Mann began to draw, not only on Adorno's manuscript, but on numerous ensuing conversations with its author when fleshing out the details, as well as constructing some of the foundations of Adrian Leverkühn's career as a composer. Adorno initiated Mann into his view of Kierkegaard, answered many musical queries posed in the elaboration of the novel (though Mann did not hesitate to seek the views of other Californian exiles, including Schoenberg and Stravinsky, when it suited him) and provided most of the instrumental and technical details of Leverkühn's fictitious compositions. Mann put many of Adorno's ideas into the mouth of Kretzschmar, as well as — a rather dubious compliment — lending his appearance to one of the guises of the devil. In *The Genesis of a Novel* Mann has expressed his indebtedness to Adorno: he even ascribed to him a prose style 'schooled by' Nietzsche (XI, 174), thus implicating his greatest mentor in one of the few aberrations of modern German culture for which he deserves no blame.

Adorno was useful to Mann at the juncture when he was trying to create a compelling motivation for Leverkühn's vocation as a composer because of his neo-marxist analysis of modern culture and his application of that understanding to contemporary music. Adorno, like other members of the Frankfurt School, tried to cope with two historical developments that raised serious objections to Marx's claim that his theories had predictive power. The first was the failure of proletarian revolution to materialise in industrialised countries, where capitalism, especially that in the USA, had raised general living standards and given workers a vested interest in maintaining a socio-economic system which delivered ever-increasing access to consumer goods. The second was the degree of mass support enjoyed by fascist movements throughout Europe, and especially in Hitler's Germany. Adorno could not settle for the comfortable but naive view espoused, for example, by Brecht, that Germany had been hijacked by a bunch of gangsters in the pay of big business and the bourgeoisie, who enjoyed no significant support among the working population. Instead, he helped develop a theory that retained Marx's materialist reinterpretation of Hegel's concept of alienation — the idea of a radical divorce, deriving from a historical process, between genuine human needs and the way society constrains people to live — while offering a grimmer view of the relationship between history, alienation and liberation. Where Marx had expected the industrial proletariat to develop a grasp of the causes of alienation and the actions needed to overcome it, Adorno and his associates described mechanisms by which the technological capabilities and rational analysis that had once promised human self-realisation had come to dominate and enslave mankind. One facet in this process was the creation of a 'culture industry' that used mass communications to stultify perception and anaesthetise dissent; and this idea led Adorno to take a very different line on modernism in art from that adopted by the theoreticians of Socialist Realism in the Soviet Union. Adorno saw the enslaving influence of the culture industry at work, not only in the blatant ideological falsifications of pulp novelettes and Hollywood movies, but also precisely in works of social criticism – such as the plays of Brecht – whose relative accessibility allowed them to contribute to mainstream debate, leading to reabsorption by the dominant ideology. For Adorno, contemporary art (and contemporary philosophy: hence the emphatically un-Nietzschean opacity of his style) had to be ferociously obscure in order to escape emasculating assimilation: relentless, well-nigh insuperable difficulty, especially formal difficulty, became for him a necessary condition of aesthetic value in the age of mass media. Music, in particular, had to 'preserve its social truth by its antithesis to society, through isolation' (*PdnM*, p. 28). At times, Adorno seems set on reversing the direction of Schiller's unease about the contrast between Kant's ethical and aesthetic doctrines. Though captivated by Kant's account of the disinterested, autonomous aesthetic object, Schiller was appalled by the rigorism of Kant's ethics and tried to recast Kant's thought into a theory that invested good deeds with the same beauty as great art. Adorno would like by contrast to make aesthetic value in the twentieth century a thing as fugitive, harsh, exacting and painful as Kantian virtue.

Under other circumstances, Mann's lifelong edginess about his own old-fashionedness would doubtless have prevented him from finding Adorno's aesthetic opinions at all congenial. There is a passage in *The Genesis of a Novel* (XI, 205) where Mann betrays his worries about not attaining the modernist reputation ascribed to James Joyce (a writer whom Mann concedes was 'linguistically inaccessible' to him, a phrase which may hint at a difficulty going beyond English vocabulary and grammar) and attempts to convince himself that many of the labels by which Harry Levin tries to encapsulate the modernism of *Ulysses* are every bit as applicable to his novels, and maybe even more so... But Adorno's account of modernism in music, which bound up artistic difficulty, isolation, alienation and austere integrity into an historical account of the ills of contemporary civilisation, came into Mann's hands precisely when he was grappling with the problem of plausibly making a great composer out of a hero whose isolation and analytical ferocity were so radical as to preclude any straightforward engagement with cultural tradition. It must have seemed a godsend of the kind he had experienced when, over forty years earlier, the discovery of Schopenhauer's reflections on personal immortality had suggested a way to dispatch Thomas Buddenbrook into the final phase of his inner decline. From the first notebook jottings of 1905, Mann's Faustian artist had been envisaged as distinctively modern in a Nietzschean sense; what Adorno's ideas provided was a way of making Leverkühn not only modern but modern*ist*, in a way that solved the conundrum of how to portray him as radically innovative in artistic means and content while simultaneously providing his creative solitude with cultural and historical roots. Both Nietzsche and Adorno were acutely suspicious of the notion of well-formed 'works' of art, regarding them as essentially fraudulent. The chief characteristic of a modern artist, according to Nietzsche's understanding, is a combination of excessive awareness and defective vitality. In Nietzsche's reckoning with Wagner, where most of his significant utterances on art and modernity are to be found, he labels his one-time friend and idol 'the modern artist *par excellence*' (Schlechta II, 913) whose secret is an 'incapacity for organic creation' (Schlechta II, 917) concealed behind a virtuoso array of tricks designed to make a 'collection of bits and pieces' (Stückwerk), laboriously strung together, look like the product of spontaneous and sustained creativity. He a 'play-actor', whose chief principle is that 'what is to have the effect of truth must not *be* true' (Schlechta II, 920). Nietzsche believed that 'the Wagner case' was not an individual aberration but the fate of anyone aiming at a semblance of artistic greatness in an age where people know too many disabling truths about themselves, their culture and their past to be able to rise to grand affirmations or expansive emotions without sacrificing their intellectual integrity. Wagner's 'play-acting', his artistic 'confidence trickery' is therefore a sign of his underlying clear-sightedness, of the accuracy of his covert perception of the modern condition and of the appropriateness, however despicable Nietzsche may find it, of his response. One strand in Leverkühn's difficulties as he hesitates on the brink of commitment to art is his reluctance to become another such prime exemplar of modernity as Nietzsche conceived it. He pens an analysis of the devices at work in the prelude to Act III of *Die Meistersinger*, prefacing it with the remark 'this is the sort of thing that goes on when something is beautiful' and is half-regretful, half proud at his own reaction, the fruit of his critical intelligence:

My dear friend, why do I have to laugh? Could anyone possibly show more genius in making use of tradition, employing all the finest tricks? Could anyone achieve beauty with greater skill at managing emotion? And I in my depravity have to laugh ... I may have tears in my eyes at the same time, but the urge to laugh carries the day.

(p. 180, LP 135)

Which leads Leverkühn to the crucial question: 'Why must it be that virtually every, no, each and every device and convention of art strikes me as *suitable nowadays only for parody*?' The question is decisive because it expresses the circumscribed choice of equally unpalatable alternatives which is all Leverkühn can see for himself, given the power of his critical intelligence: if compose he must, he has to choose between confidence trickery or a parody, either cynically manipulating conventions to hoodwink the naive, or ingeniously exaggerating them to entertain the initiated (the 'aristocratic nihilism' of parody about which the devil will speak). The creation of 'organic' works of art presupposes a vitality of inspiration and a freedom from disabling self-consciousness which he sees, at this juncture, no way of attaining.

Deliberate contraction of a disease that would free the Faustian artist from intellectual inhibition by progressively destroying his rational self was the solution to this dilemma which Mann had envisaged from the earliest conception of the plot. But under Adorno's influence he added a further ingredient to the problem which required a significant additional component in the attempted solution.

Adorno was every bit as suspicious as Nietzsche of the notion of the ample, well-formed, harmonious work of art in the modern age. But where Nietzsche saw defective vitality and excessive consciousness as the enemies of the 'work', Adorno claimed that such 'works' implied a view of culture and society which was no longer valid. Adorno saw the claim to large-scale, orderly, comprehensive and comprehensible structure as the site of a 'work's' essential falsehood, since this structure made a spurious claim to draw upon and reflect an analogous social order. As Adorno writes:

> The sickness which has befallen the idea of the 'work' doubtless stems from a state of society which holds out nothing sufficiently binding and established to underwrite the harmony of the self-sufficient work. (*PdnM*, pp. 42–3)

Or, as Zeitblom puts it, claiming to be paraphrasing and synthesising various remarks made to him by Leverkühn, but in fact being made to weave together the two strands, one from Nietzsche, the other from Adorno, behind the novel's notion of the unviability of the traditional musical 'work':

> There is a great deal that is illusory about a work of art, one could go further and say that it is, precisely *as* a 'work', intrinsically illusory. It aspires to create the belief that it was not made, but simply sprang into existence, like ... Pallas Athene ... from Jupiter's head. But that is pretence ... It is the product of labour, artistic labour aimed at producing semblance – and the question arises whether in the present state of our consciousness, our knowledge, our sense of truth, this game is still permissible, ... can still be taken seriously, whether [and here is the point in this line of thought where Nietzsche gives way to Adorno] the work as such, as a self-sufficient, harmoniously self-contained creation, still stands in any legitimate relationship to the altogether uncertain, problematic and inharmonious state of our social circumstances, whether all semblance, even the most beautiful, indeed precisely the most beautiful has not in our day become a *lie*.
> (p. 240, LP 183–4)

An artist who wishes to escape a silence enforced by integrity must find a mode of utterance which makes no claims to referential or analogical truth, a kind of composition that openly proclaims, rather than implicitly denies, the artist's alienation from a chaotic and inhuman world. That is why Leverkühn is made to devise serialism as the second essential component, alongside syphilitic infection, of his distinctive, 'demonic' path to musical greatness.

Demonic relations

The link between syphilitic infection and inspiration – to concentrate first on the earlier component in the scheme – is a special case of Mann's lifelong preoccupation with the existential and symbolic significance of 'illness', fuelled both by his reading of Nietzsche's works and by rather sensational versions of Nietzsche's biography to which he lent uncritical credence. He accepted the notion that Nietzsche's symptoms were syphilitic, believed contentious accounts according to which Nietzsche knowingly contracted the disease, and took it for granted that there was an essential link between the progression of this assumed clinical condition and the entire content and the development of Nietzsche's thought, with the eventual insanity as the last stage in a long-drawn-out pathological process. Leverkühn would accordingly seek release from the stranglehold of his critical intelligence in a disease which he knew would eventually destroy his mind, in the (more or less vindicated) belief that in the intervening period between infection and breakdown he will enjoy a period of increasingly exuberant creative energy – a notion that did not seem so preposterously implausible to Mann as it has always done to many readers. All the same, he does not portray Leverkühn coolly deciding he needs some pathological assistance and nonchalantly going off to obtain it. On the contrary, for all the crudely instrumental function which Leverkühn's illness performs in his biography, there is nothing pragmatic or calculating about the actions which lead to his infection: they are woven into a tissue of motivations involving psychological tensions already established in the account of his childhood and adolescence. He acts under irrational impulse, though the novel is constructed so that from a broader perspective, that impulse makes sense.

Leverkühn's involuntary introduction to the prostitute he will later deliberately seek out comes on the evening of his arrival in Leipzig to begin his musical studies, when the guide he has hired to show him the city leads him to end the day in a brothel instead of a restaurant. In outline and in many of its details, the incident is modelled on an anecdote from Nietzsche's life. But the broader context created by the way the episode is narrated belongs very much to the distinctive quality of this work. This is, in fact, one of only two sections in the novel where Leverkühn himself performs the narration, in a document which Zeitblom cites verbatim (the other is, of course, his account of the dialogue with the devil). Both these narratives, though in Leverkühn's own words, are not actually in his normal voice, the generally laconic and sober tones we find in his various quoted utterances: they are in a mock-antique diction modelled on the sixteenth-century German of the *Faust-buch* and Luther's Bible, a diction which Leverkühn finally adopts once more when introducing his last work and summing up his life as a series of Faustian transgressions. Zeitblom explains this strange mannerism as an attempt to embed the account in a particular atmosphere, which he labels 'religious'. The broader implications of what Zeitblom means by 'religious', here and elsewhere, will be considered later; the immediate significance of the term here has to do with Zeitblom's sense that this apparently trivial incident strikes to the very foundations of Leverkühn's selfhood. It brings him 'a profound disturbance, an experience of profundity' (p. 239, LP 182) (ein Erlebnis von Tiefe) because it engages with the underlying tensions of an existence that is lacking in 'soul' and knows only the tension between extremes: intellectual rigour and raw instinctual drives. All the power of desire undeveloped and unaccommodated in his past is unleashed and becomes centred on the woman who 'touched' him, the 'brunette with... almond eyes' whom he names Esmeralda (p. 191, LP 143), thus aligning her with his father's 'ambiguous' speculations, for *hetaera esmeralda* was the scientific name of one of the exotic insects illustrated in Johann Leverkühn's books. 'Spiritual arrogance had suffered the trauma of encountering soulless instinct' (p. 198, LP 150) is Zeitblom's commentary on the incident, and is also the core of his explanation for the fact that Leverkühn found himself compelled to return with the intention of completing the encounter from which he had only temporarily fled. Beyond Zeitblom's awareness, however, there is a suggestion of more unfinished (or even unstarted) erotic business at stake than he imagines, a dimension to what he terms the 'terrifyingly symbolic' (p. 197, LP 149) character of the encounter which eludes him.

Much ado is made in this novel about the colour of people's eyes and its importance to Leverkühn. The only direct description of any aspect of his appearance concerns his eye colour, which we are told is a 'mixture of grey, blue and green', with 'a rust-coloured ring around the pupils' (p. 228, LP 174). Zeitblom says his friend had 'a strong sensitivity to the human eye', 'a receptivity, indeed a weakness for its charms' (p. 236, LP 180), and more than once remarks that the three people who seemed to mean most to him had eyes that were either blue (his nephew Echo and Schwerdtfeger the violinist, who was able to draw him into a brief homosexual relationship) or black (Marie Godeau, to whom Leverkühn proposes marriage). So it is noticeable that although 'Esmeralda''s eyes figure prominently in the brief sketch of her appearance which Leverkühn provides, the phrase he uses indicates only their shape and conceals their colour. That it is a matter of concealment rather than of indifference emerges from Leverkühn's reflection of the impact of 'Esmeralda' through his opera based on *Love's Labour's Lost*. Zeitblom leaves us in no doubt that Leverkühn is fascinated by '[Berowne's] despair at his emotional subjection to [Rosaline]' because he sees here, in this depiction of 'gravity's revolt to wantonness' an image of his own tormented preoccupation with 'Esmeralda'. His anguish finds expression in the distinctive leitmotif his score associates with every mention of Rosaline's eyes, culminating in a 'half lyrical-passionate, half grotesque melisma' at Berowne's line 'O, but her eye − by this light, but for her eye I would not love her' (p. 287, LP 219).

But Rosaline's eyes are 'pitch black', and so, we may infer, are those of 'Esmeralda'. This matters because there is yet another pair of black eyes, strangely missing from Zeitblom's lists of blue and black-eyed people in Leverkühn's life, but identified all the same in an apparently off-hand phrase (p. 172, LP 129): they belong to his mother, Elsbeth Leverkühn, who 'forbade' herself those musical predispositions which the text associates with desire. Part of the 'terrifying symbolism' of the encounter with 'Esmeralda' and its consequences is that it is a figure of incest.

This lends a disconcerting undertone to Zeitblom's well-meaning attempts to argue that Leverkühn's 'defeat at the hands of naked instinct' in returning to the brothel was not 'devoid of all human ennoblement' (p. 204, LP 155), for Zeitblom's argument turns on an insistence that Leverkühn *chose* this woman rather than any other, tracking her down to Preßburg (now Bratislava, though for mischievous reasons, Mann has Zeitblom tell us its Hungarian name). It also provides, at a deeper level than Zeitblom's conscious awareness, an origin for that 'tremor of religious awe' which he says seizes him whenever he thinks of the ensuing sexual embrace. For the motif of symbolic incest in the cause of breaking out of intellectual sterility does not appear among the references which Zeitblom uses to underpin his 'elevation' of the episode. He focuses instead on the implications of 'Esmeralda''s warning to Leverkühn against the enjoyment of her body and his insistence on 'possessing this flesh' despite, or maybe even because of, the knowledge of the likelihood of infection. The warning was, Zeitblom reflects, 'a free spiritual act by which she rose above her wretched physical condition ... an act of love'. As to Leverkühn's reasons for ignoring it, Zeitblom resorts to a series of perhaps not wholly rhetorical questions, reflecting not just confusion or indecision, but an elusive sense that the whole episode defies categorisation:

Was it not also love on his part, or what was it then, what obsession, what determination to tempt God by a reckless act, what compulsion to make the punishment part of the sin, or finally: what deep, intensely

secret longing for demonic conception, for a chemical alteration of
his nature both liberating and deadly, made him spurn the warning...?
(p. 206, LP 157)

The speculation that there may have been some element in
Leverkühn's motivation that makes it not wholly inappropriate
to talk of love gains some support from the composer's later
remarks in connection with his sister's wedding, in a conversation that will also bring the first exposition of his serial theory:

Lust for another's flesh means overcoming barriers that are otherwise
always present, barriers based on the remoteness of the 'I' from
the 'you', of the self from the other ... When the other suddenly
becomes an object of desire and lust, the relationship between 'I'
and 'you' is transformed in a fashion for which 'sensuality' is
only an empty name. You simply cannot help bringing in the notion
of love, even if there's allegedly nothing spiritual at work.
(p. 250, LP 190–1)

What seems partly the satisfaction of an obsessive lust stemming
from psychological deprivation, partly the calculating choice
of infection in the interests of creativity is imbued by these
remarks of Leverkühn's – 'he had never before abandoned
his reserve like this', his friend comments (p. 251, LP 191) –
as well as through Zeitblom's commentary, with a significance
that allows the vocabulary of salvation to be used at precisely
this moment which, under another aspect, both Leverkühn and
Zeitblom see as the making of a diabolical pact:

I have never been able to think without a tremor of religious awe
about that embrace, in which one party forfeited salvation and the
other gained it. It must have purified, justified, elevated that wretched
woman that the man who had journeyed so far refused to renounce
her possession despite the danger ... He had reason enough not to
forget her; but, although he never saw her again, he also always
remembered her for her own sake, and her name – the one he had
given her from the start – haunts his work in runic ciphers noticed
by no-one apart from myself.   (pp. 206–7, LP 157)

Zeitblom's self-congratulation here sets off his imperceptive-
ness in a closely related matter: the 'invisible figure' of Frau
von Tolna, whom Mann has associated, over Zeitblom's head,
with an array of clues that she is probably none other than
'Esmeralda' herself. The most important of these clues is an

unmistakeable indication of symbolic marriage. This rich widow of a Hungarian nobleman with a dissolute past, suffering from a chronic illness which requires her to be attended by her personal doctor wherever she goes (p. 520, LP 400), sends Leverkühn an emerald ring in which is engraved a winged monster with an arrow-shaped tongue. The connection between the stone and 'Esmeralda' is not quite so obvious in German, where 'emerald' is 'Smaragd'; and Zeitblom is not allowed to spot the link between the motif of the arrow and the encounter with 'Esmeralda', even though he is responsible for making it visible through a remark which is, in its immediate context, apparently gratuitous. During his reflections on the 'elevating' elements in Leverkühn's union with 'Esmeralda', he is made to ponder the thought that 'here, love and poison were fused into a terrible experiential unity: the mythological unity which is embodied in the *arrow*'(p. 206, LP 156), unwittingly signalling the significance of his remark by otherwise unmotivated italics. Zeitblom does not mention the existence of Frau von Tolna until he is narrating the genesis of Leverkühn's first masterpiece, the *Apocalipsis cum figuris*, composed in 1919; but he then reveals that Leverkühn had been exchanging letters with her 'for a number of years', in a correspondence that revealed her as 'a caring friend and adviser, a devoted servant of his existence' and in which he in return 'went to the limit of communication and trust of which a solitary person is capable' (p. 519, LP 399). It was with the very first of her letters, we learn, that she sent the ring; and since then Leverkühn has 'observed the custom, or should I say the ritual, of putting it on while he worked' (p. 522, LP 401). Though Zeitblom observes that a ring is 'a symbol of a bond, a fetter, indeed the mark of profound dependency' he is quite unconcerned about the implications of his further reflection that Frau von Tolna doubtless saw herself in the role of a mother-figure (p. 521, LP 400). All this envelops the original motif of deliberately sought syphilitic infection in layers of further meaning that muffle its essential crudity and implausibility. The union with a prostitute acquires elements of symbolic incest and symbolic marriage, and becomes an emblem of both damnation and salvation.

Though it belongs to a much later stage in the conception of the novel, the second component in Leverkühn's forging of a distinct musical style, his invention of serial technique, is made to grow out of this same primal 'Esmeralda'-experience. The 'runic ciphers' in which 'Esmeralda''s memory haunts Leverkühn's work consist of the repeated occurrence of a particular note-sequence, B, E, A, E, E flat, which in German nomenclature spell out h e a e es, for hetaera esmeralda. In his conversation with Zeitblom after his sister's wedding, Leverkühn expounds twelve-note serialism taking his use of this motif in his setting of a Brentano poem as a starting point:

[The setting] is entirely derived from a basic structure, a sequence of intervals with many possible variations, the five notes B, E, A, E, E flat. Harmony and melody are governed and determined by it, as far as that is possible with a basic motif with so few notes. It's like a word, a key word, whose traces are to be found everywhere in the song ... The thing to do would be to develop this and form longer words from the twelve notes of the tempered chromatic scale, words with twelve letters, particular combinations and interconnections of the twelve semitones, note-rows from which the piece, the individual movement or an entire work in several movements could be strictly derived. Every note in the entire composition, in melody and harmony, would have to establish its credentials in relation to this predetermined underlying series ... Not a single free note would remain. That's what I would call rigorous composition.   (pp. 258–9, LP 194–5)

This particular path to serial technique is, of course, very much part of Mann's invented world, and Schoenberg's subsequent chagrin at what he saw as the theft of his intellectual property is understandable enough. But the account of twelve-note serialism itself, and the broader historical derivation which Leverkühn provides for it, is heavily indebted to Adorno's discussion of Schoenberg's path from chromaticism to composition by note-row, from which it makes extensive verbatim borrowings (*PdnM*, pp. 55–66). It traces the origins of serialism as a method of organisation back to the treatment of sonata form by Beethoven and Brahms, with their wish to organise their works, not by reliance on traditional forms, but from the resources of their own artistic inventiveness. This they did by expanding the development section. What had once been

'a minor part of the sonata, a modest space where the dynamics
... of subjectivity could have free rein', became in their hands

universal, the centre of the entire form ... Where there is nothing
unthematic left, nothing that cannot establish its credentials as a
derivation from an unchanging identity, it is scarcely possible to talk
any longer of free composition. (pp. 254–5, LP 194)

So Beethoven and Brahms, making variations upon motifs of
their own choosing into the organisational principle of their
works, furnish the prime examples of modern individualism
in music. But their freedom from constraints outside their own
creativity proved problematic:

Freedom is after all just another word for subjectivity, and there
comes a time when subjectivity becomes weary of its own company,
despairs of being able to be creative from its own resources, and seeks
protection and security in something objective. (p. 253, LP 193)

The 'objectivity' Leverkühn has in mind is the use of the tone-
row to furnish the raw material upon which the composer goes
to work. Replacement of the individually invented motif by
the arbitrarily chosen tone-row is, from this perspective, only
a minor change: the character of the composer's organising
activities and the skills of motivic variation on which they
draw remain essentially unaltered. But from the perspective
of the listener who had not grasped the intensely subjective
character of Beethoven's or Brahms's art because of the familiar
tonal material in which it was exercised, the transition to serial
atonality is a bewildering shock. The isolation of the modern
artist, previously masked by tonal continuities, is now openly
proclaimed through the immediate acoustic impact of the atonal
work and is sustained when even protracted listening fails to
produce patterns that engage reliably with tonal expectations.
The work's organisation has passed from being covertly to
demonstratively arcane, the modernist work emphasises its
own difficulty in its programmatic refusal to mirror a spurious
community of shared values and meanings.

Two components in his friend's programme strike Zeitblom
as an affront to humane ideals and so 'barbaric'. First, the
recourse to an arbitrary numerical series for the basic material,

which looks to Zeitblom dangerously like an abandonment of Enlightenment in the classical Kantian sense, a cult of the irrational in preference to human powers of decision and choice:

The rationality you call for has a strong element of superstition about it, the belief in intangible and vaguely demonic powers of the kind that has its way in games of chance, in divination by cards and dice, in casting runes. (p. 258, LP 197)

Secondly, Zeitblom is suspicious of the notion of the composer being 'liberated' from subjectivity by submitting to the rigid discipline of the note-row. Leverkühn claims that this is simply a 'dialectical' redefinition of freedom:

Freedom soon rediscovers itself within constraint, fulfils itself in submission to laws, rules, compulsion, the demands of a system — fulfils itself, which means it doesn't for all that stop being freedom.

Zeitblom is unimpressed, for this smacks of the totalitarian claim to coerce people into freedom for their own good:

That's what it [i.e. freedom] thinks! ... But in reality it isn't freedom any longer, any more than a dictatorship born of revolution is still freedom. (p. 254, LP 193)

Wilful irrationality and conscious abandonment of liberal individualism: these are the two things that Zeitblom identifies as 'barbaric' in Leverkühn's technique (and will rediscover in significant aspects of the works which that technique makes possible). Leverkühn does not share his disquiet. The choice of 'barbarity' in the interests of replacing an effete 'civilisation' by a dynamic 'culture' is very much part of Leverkühn's rationale for inventing serialism, so that his friend's scruples and fears confirm him in his purpose rather than deterring him from it.

By the end of Section XXII of the novel, then, Mann has completed the course of Leverkühn's development into an artist who is Nietzschean in his resort to a pathological stimulus that can liberate creativity from the constraints of excessive consciousness, and who is a thoroughgoing modernist in his espousal of a technique of composition which, as a matter of artistic integrity, flaunts its inaccessibility. The making of the Faustian artist is complete. He is twenty-five, and his sister's wedding, which provides the occasion for his exposition of twelve-note theory, is the last time he sees his parents or his home before his collapse into insanity twenty years later. Everything else that follows in his life story is the relentless working-out of the decisions he has already made and priorities he has long since set himself.

A dialogue with destiny

Adrian Leverkühn's conversation with the devil in Section XXV of the novel does not send the plot in a decisively new direction. Its place in the work's economy resembles Ivan's encounter with Satan in Dostoyevsky's *The Brothers Karamazov* more than the dramatic pact scenes of the *Faust* tradition. Like Ivan, Leverkühn in talking to the devil is not initiating a decisive new turn in his career, but exploring the 'diabolical' components in things in his long-standing priorities. His infection has been acquired some four years earlier, and his serial technique has been fully thought out, if not yet consistently applied, by the time Leverkühn decides to spend a time outside Germany, in a place where he can 'hold converse with [his] destiny', the Italian villa where, one night, the devil appears to him.

The ensuing dialogue reviews his motives for contracting syphilis, airs the hoped-for creative gains and holds them against the anticipated costs, revealing strong undercurrents of anxiety. For example, the devil alludes more than once to the 'osmotic growths' in Johann Leverkühn's crystal garden. The commonplace chemical experiment is described at length in Zeitblom's account of Leverkühn's childhood with a pathos which, at the time, seems gratuitous. The crystal growths, Johann Leverkühn solemnly tells the children,

are not plants, they're just pretending to be. But don't think any the worse of them for that. The way they pretend and try their very best deserves every respect.

(This is not, alas, the point at which his son laughs: Adrian's characteristic amusement comes later, at a rather less fatuous juncture.) And Zeitblom's commentary takes up this incongruous note of anxious solicitude for this 'pitiable brood':

> It emerged that these growths were of definitely inorganic origin, brought into being with the aid of substances from the apothecary's shop ... [Johann Leverkühn] showed us that these wretched imitators of living things were hungry for light, 'heliotropic' ... He exposed the aquarium to sunshine ... and sure enough, the whole dubious tribe... soon began leaning towards the side of the glass container through which the light was passing ... with such an intense yearning for warmth and joy that they practically flattened themselves against the glass and clung fast to it.   (p. 31, LP 18)

There is here an obvious overdetermination of the whole motif and its details: this inflation of a mildly curious phenomenon with heavy emotional connotations has no clear function at this point in the story. When the devil takes up the motif, however, in the context of Leverkühn's desperate quest for creativity, the significance of this inordinate compassion is revealed. It has to do with the suspicion, obscurely raised in the very first pages of the novel, that Leverkühn's 'genius' is not 'pure and genuine, a gift or a burden bestowed by God', but on the contrary 'dubiously acquired and destructive', the product of the 'sinful and morbid combustion of natural gifts' in fulfilment of a 'horrendous contract'(p. 11, LP 2). So the devil's promise that 'osmotic growths' will sprout up out of what Leverkühn has 'planted' is anything but reassuring (p. 313, LP 239). It reinforces Leverkühn's fears that 'gold made by fire and not by the sun is not genuine' (p.315, LP 240). Sure enough, it holds out the prospect of creativity liberated by the effects of disease, but raises the suspicion that the products of that creativity will stand to expressions of 'pure and genuine' genius as the crystal growths stand to real plants. No matter how intense his efforts and how fervent his aspiration towards 'warmth' and 'light', there is the risk that Leverkühn's works may remain a 'dubious bunch', unable to conceal their 'inorganic' origins. This fear is woven still tighter into the texture of his self-understanding when the devil goes on to apply the motif of osmosis to the pathology of Leverkühn's infection, explaining that liquid diffusion is the key to the progress of the syphilis bacteria through the nervous system (p. 313, LP 239). And Leverkühn will remember this point, with the question mark it places against the value of his achievement, when he encounters the same osmotic process at work in the death of his nephew from meningitis (p. 632, LP 488).

The devil insists that he always keeps his promises (p. 301, LP 230) but the reassurance rings more than a little hollow when he characterises the inspiration that Leverkühn will gain in terms borrowed from Nietzsche's description, in his manic autobiography *Ecce homo*, of the state of 'illumination' in which he wrote *Zarathustra*:

> an inspiration where there is no choice, no correcting and tinkering, where everything is received like an enraptured dictation ... a man so visited is swept from head to toe by sublime tremors, a torrent of joyful tears bursts from his eyes.   (p. 317, LP 242)

What makes this promise fishy is a point made by Thomas Mann himself in his essay 'Nietzsche's Philosophy in the Light of our Experience' (IX, 675–712) published in 1947, and described by him as an 'essayistic epilogue' to this novel (XI, 300). Alluding to the same passage from *Ecce homo*, he points out that Nietzsche is 'blindly overestimating' the value of what he wrote in his creative ecstasy, and goes on to give his description of Zarathustra in terms which have striking affinities to Zeitblom's characterisation of the 'osmotic growths':

> This faceless and formless monster ... Zarathustra ... is not an artistic creation, he is mere rhetoric, feverish verbal wit ... a pitifully grandiloquent shell, often touching, mostly embarrassing – a non-character teetering on the brink of the ridiculous.   (IX, 682)

So the devil's promises about the 'feelings of power and glory' of 'triumphant well-being' which will alternate with periods of sterility and pain concern only Leverkühn's subjective condition. That the works produced in those exalted states do eventually prove to be masterpieces is far from guaranteed in this dialogue, making them, in consequence, a product of Leverkühn's individual achievement, unsullied by their 'diabolical' preconditions. As the devil also says: 'We create nothing new ... We simply unbind and set free. We make lameness and shyness, chaste scruples and doubts go to blazes' (p. 315, LP 241). That, more modest, promise is certainly kept.

The devil makes a second promise, corresponding to a further dimension of Leverkühn's hopes. It concerns the place Leverkühn's works will have in the broader history of music in particular and culture in general. This is a question that matters very much to Leverkühn, for Kretzschmar has taught him to find his vocation in taking art out of its present impasse. The devil assures him that his 'sickness' will bring 'health' to others:

We vouch for the vitalising effectiveness of what you will produce with our aid. You will lead the way ... your name will be sacred to all the fellows who thanks to your madness will not need to be mad themselves. You will not simply break through the disabling difficulties of the age – you will break through the age itself, the cultural epoch, that is to say the epoch of culture and the cult of culture, and dare to achieve barbarity, a double barbarity, since it follows upon humanity and ... liberal refinement.   (p. 324, LP 247)

This promise will appear to be kept, as we shall see, in the first of Adrian Leverkühn's great works, *Apocalipsis cum figuris*, where the 'breakthrough' to highly sophisticated barbarity is indeed achieved. But that work is not the culmination of Leverkühn's career, nor are its implications the last word about his place in the broader scheme of cultural history. Leverkühn will become far less sanguine about the rejuvenating effects of 'barbarity': and his last work, *The Lamentation of Dr Faustus*, will be a complex mixture of both affirmation and repudiation of the course he has chosen and the works it has enabled him to produce. The groundwork for the shift in attitude, which will be explored through the motif of 'repentance', is likewise laid in the conversation with the devil, in the last two stages where Leverkühn asks about the nature of Hell and 'learns' of a significant prohibition that is part of his 'contract' with demonic powers.

The motivation for Leverkühn's curiosity about hell goes beyond his individual psychology. Partly, Mann is offering a parallel to the stratagems by which Ivan Karamazov tries to get his diabolical visitor to unmask himself as a hallucination by challenging him to supply information that Ivan himself could not have known. As in Dostoyevsky's novel, the conundrum of the devil's status as hallucination or reality is an essential ingredient in the work's meaning which will be examined later. In a fashion reminiscent of the 'occult' episode in *The Magic Mountain*, which culminates in an apparition of the hero's cousin Joachim Ziemßen, not in the glamorous Prussian uniform in which he was buried, but in the drab battledress of the First World War which has yet to be devised at the moment when his ghostly form is witnessed by the séance, the devil is made to characterise hell in 'clairvoyant' terms closely akin to those Thomas Mann used, thirty-four years after this dialogue ostensibly takes place, to speak to his listeners in an all-but-defeated Germany of the atrocities discovered when the extermination camps were liberated. Then again, the curiosity about hell, like the cosmic journeys which Leverkühn will later pretend to have made, belongs to the enactment of the *Faustbuch* paradigm in which Leverkühn as character, as well as Mann as author, is consciously engaged. Finally, the evocations of infernal torment allow the devil to voice a suspicion about Leverkühn's reasons for requesting them which introduces what is, in effect, the only significantly new element which this section of the novel has to contribute to the thematic scheme — the idea of different kinds of remorse and their validity:

> You are intent on interrogating me so as to fill yourself with dread, dread of hell. For in the background you harbour a thought of turning back, of escape, of the so-called salvation of your soul ... you are striving to summon up the attritio cordis, the heartfelt fear of that place, of which you may have heard tell that it can earn men so-called eternal bliss. Believe me, that is utterly outdated theology.
>
> (p. 328, LP 251)

This, too, is a reference to the *Faustbuch* and its specifically Lutheran theological framework which will be considered more fully when the novel's religious and moral dimensions are under review.

The final facet of the review of Leverkühn's past and prospects which this episode enacts through the image of ratifying a diabolical pact is the issue of the price to be paid. The earlier sections of the dialogue have allowed glimpses of Leverkühn's anxiety about the artistic worth of the works he hopes to create as a consequence of his infection, his unease about whether gold made with demonic fire can be minted into coinage that rings true. The parting exchanges with his gruesome visitor hint at a similarly nagging disquiet about the full cost of this problematic creative enrichment. The devil summarises the terms of the 'pact':

Time we have granted you, time filled with genius, time that will raise you to the heights, a full twenty-four years ab dato recessi ... When that time is over ... you will be fetched. We for our part will mean-times be obedient and beholden to you in all things, and hell shall cause your doings to prosper, if you but renounce all living beings, all the host of heaven and all mankind, for it must be so.

(p.331, LP 253)

Leverkühn records feeling 'an extremely chill blast' at these words and exclaims 'What? That's something new. What does that clause mean?' (p.331, LP 253). A most striking reaction this. Leverkühn clearly knows his *Faustbuch* very well, so it is remarkable to find him reacting with surprise and describing as 'new' a 'clause' which is a verbatim quotation from the text of Faust's pact in the sixteenth-century source. It signals that the devil has here touched upon a matter which Leverkühn would prefer not to dwell upon, a part of his 'destiny' which he would rather not acknowledge. Sure enough, the devil proceeds to gloss this prohibition in a way without precedent in the *Faustbuch*, but which bears very strongly upon Leverkühn's most characteristic traits of personality. 'Love is forbidden you', the devil explains, 'insofar as it brings warmth' (p. 332, LP 254). He must expect to pay some price before his final collapse for the benefits he will receive; and this price is the complete renunciation of emotional 'warmth', something which the devil, speaking to the man with 'not much "soul"', can dismiss as in any case of little worth (p. 332, LP 254).

The radical solitude which drove Leverkühn to his musical destiny in the first place must never be breached. Any attempt to do so would be a violation of the 'contract' through which his creativity has been unlocked, and would put that creativity in jeopardy:

> We want to keep you cold, so that the flames of composition will scarcely be hot enough to bring you warmth. You will take refuge in them from the coldness of your life.   (p. 332, LP 254)

These considerations will underpin the experiences of his last few years of sanity, which will be aligned with the episode of the pious neighbour's call to repentance in the *Faustbuch*, and they will also enter into the complex judgement he passes on such 'temptations' to 'repentance', both in his last masterpiece and in his self-assessment before his final collapse.

Society and solitude

The remainder of the novel, concerned with the working out of that destiny which Leverkühn had anxiously reviewed in his dialogue with the devil, brings a certain split in narrative focus. Up to this point, Leverkühn himself has been very much at the centre of things, with other people and circumstances introduced and pursued only insofar as they had a direct bearing on his existence. That held good for the account of the people with whom he came into contact after first moving to Munich. Zeitblom provided us with a brief introduction to the Rodde family with whom Leverkühn lodges, and to the circle of musicians and artists, including the violinist Rudi Schwerdt-feger, with whom he came into contact via the Rodde house-hold. None of these figures was, however, followed very far outside Leverkühn's immediate awareness. On his return from Italy, however, Leverkühn elects not to return to the city but to move to the Schweigestills' farm with its uncanny resemblance to his childhood surroundings, and from here on the fortunes of the people in the Munich circles where he is only sporadically present are developed much more extensively, giving the plot a new centre of gravity some way to one side of Leverkühn's solitary creative existence. For a dozen years, between his move to Pfeiffering and the beginning of his liaison with Schwerdt-feger, the only significant events in Leverkühn's life are his intensely private musical struggles and triumphs, which Zeitblom describes in the intervals of his accounts of more eventful lives which occupy the narrative foreground for much of the time.

1912 sees the completion of *Love's Labour's Lost*, while the following year brings Lieder to poems by Blake and Keats and *Frühlingsfeyer*, a setting for baritone, organ and strings of a poem by Klopstock. In 1914 he completes the orchestral fantasia *Wunder des Alls* and a puppet opera based on episodes from the *Gesta Romanorum*. There follows a period of severe illness and creative sterility, from which he recovers in 1919 to write the first of his two masterpieces, *Apocalipsis cum figuris*. In the meantime, cataclysms shake the world outside his rural retreat, apparently with no significant impact upon him. Most important of these are, of course, the World War and the ensuing revolution and hyperinflation, events in which Leverkühn shows scant interest. Zeitblom, however, will narrate the genesis and describe the structure of the *Apocalipsis* in ways that establish the strongest possible links between Leverkühn's creative imagination and the historical-political sphere to which he seems so indifferent. There are also, in these twelve years, disasters and upheavals a-plenty in the personal realm of the Munich characters about whom we now learn so much more, in a way that at first appears to have little bearing either on Leverkühn's interests or on his work. We follow the accelerating decline of the Rodde family, with the mother, 'widow of a Senator from Bremen', slowly sinking into morphine addiction while her daughters also come to grief. Clara, the younger child, desperately tries to make a career as an actress, despite her nagging awareness that she lacks the necessary talent (p. 380, LP 290). We learn of successes 'more erotic than artistic in character' (p. 461, LP 354), of the chance of a marriage wrecked by a malicious blackmailer, and of her eventual suicide in 1922. (In what might be thought a rather questionable application of his 'montage' technique, Thomas Mann was here recreating

very closely the life and death of one of his own sisters.) Her
elder sister, Ines, is also determined to escape the slightly gamey
milieu of her mother's semi-bohemian salon, but her personality
takes her in the opposite direction, the quest for a highly conventional marriage in the best upper-middle-class manner,
where she can be 'rich, well-provided for and cushioned against
life' (p. 434, LP 333). She finds a husband whose interest in
such a marriage is as suspect as her own: Helmut Institoris,
art-historian, aesthete and tubercular admirer of 'everything
reckless and brutally vital', who wants to 'found a household
where members of high society will meet' for reasons of
personal ambition, and who also, as a 'regular client of a
sanatorium for rich patients in Meran', hopes that marriage
will improve his health (p.382, LP 292). Zeitblom witnesses and
muses upon the way Ines begins, shortly after her wedding in
1915, a long-drawn-out and increasingly less discreet turbulent
affair with Rudi Schwerdtfeger, and has to suffer being, in
turn, the confidant of both the lovers. In particular, he observes
with growing unease Ines' intense jealousy towards Schwerdtfeger, a passion which will eventually have a violent outcome
that also reveals links between Adrian Leverkühn and all these
goings on, even though he seems remote from them. The murder
of Schwerdtfeger by Ines Rodde is the indirect consequence
of Leverkühn's partial and brief emergence from isolation in
1924, venturing first on a relationship with Schwerdtfeger and
then even making a proposal of marriage to the Swiss stage
designer, Marie Godeau. After these sallies out of his radical
solitude have come to an abrupt end with a bloody aftermath,
Leverkühn again withdraws into isolation for the last phase of
his life, and this time the narrative perspective follows him.
The relatively wider world of Munich fades into the background
for the episode of his nephew Echo's arrival and harrowing
death, and appears only once more, when its surviving members
are summoned by Leverkühn to be introduced to his last work
and witness his taking stock of his existence.

Apocalypse

The first high point of Leverkühn's creative life comes with the composition of the *Apocalipsis cum figuris*. This work, and its detailed description over three long sections, intertwined with an account of the climate in Munich intellectual circles immediately after the First World War, is made to carry a heavy load of significance, part of which will be examined later in the context of the novel's historical themes and claims. Considered from the point of view of Leverkühn's personal development, it represents dramatic evidence of the 'pact' paying off. Though its composition is preceded by months of physical illness and mental torment at the apparent drying-up of his inventiveness, these prove to be merely the intense 'cold' out of which, as the devil promised, Leverkühn dramatically passes into the feverish 'heat' of a creativity far more exuberant and imperious than anything he has previously known when, in the spring of 1919, 'his spirit arose to supreme freedom and an astonishing power of uninhibited, not to say ruthless productivity' (p.468, LP 359). This is strikingly different from the arduous assembly of 'bits and pieces' into the semblance of a whole which Mann, following Nietzsche, believed to be the inescapable lot of a modern creator of a 'work' on the grand scale. It is the overweening, imperious inspiration for which Leverkühn had bartered his 'soul', and it is shown in productive engagement with the compositional technique applied by his mind, whose inhibiting hold over his imagination has been broken by the advance of the disease. The abundance of expansive melodic ideas is visited upon him, but he does not remain a passive recipient. Before they are built into the composition, these themes are 're-thought' as note-rows, submitted to a ruthless intellectual discipline, their 'fire' tempered and 'cooled' by the relentless rigour of his serial technique. All this is described in terms which strongly connote violence and pain. The melodic ideas are 'inflicted upon' Leverkühn, he in turn 'coerces' them into shape in a process which Zeitblom finds most unpleasant to witness, particularly since it disfigures his friend's face, suggesting that Leverkühn's nature is being as much violated as fulfilled in this, his hour of creative triumph (p. 478, LP 366). There are echoes of Kretzschmar's account of Beethoven's 'wrestling with the angel' over the fugal passages of the *Missa Solemnis* (p. 80, LP 56), but here the outcome of the struggle is itself replete with desperation and anguish. The concluding section, 'far removed from the music of Romantic redemption, implacably confirms the theologically negative and merciless character of the whole work' (p. 479, LP 368). In particular, a distinctive deployment of tonality aggressively asserts the connection between truth and radical austerity:

the entire work is dominated by the paradox (if it is indeed a paradox) that within it dissonance stands for the expression of everything lofty, serious, pious and spiritual, whereas tonal and harmonic elements are reserved for the world of hell, in this case therefore a world of the banal and the commonplace.   (p. 498, LP 382)

Instruments and voices are treated in such a way that 'the boundary between human beings and inanimate things seems to be shifted', the tenor-narrator has to eschew any resemblance to *bel canto* and produce a tone that is 'cold and croaking', and the 'spine-chilling' and regressive use of glissando given to the human voice, 'which was after all the first place where tonal order emerged, bringing liberation from primeval howling' (p. 497, LP 382) completes the impression that the work is both summing up and mocking the entire Western musical tradition, its contents as well as its forms. It is not just the texts, inspired by Dürer's woodcut illustrations of the Book of Revelation, and drawing on a wide range of other apocalyptic sources, which make the oratorio what Zeitblom terms 'a résumé of all proclamations of the End' (p. 475, LP 364): it embodies in its musical means and their organisation the repudiation of humanist individualism and its artistic analogues, and so represents that venture into barbarism which the devil so problematically foretold.

Zeitblom rehearses all the grounds on which the work can be accused of barbarity and 'soullessness' but insists that there are other elements as well which point in a different direction, even though they occur only in fleeting passages of lyricism 'which could bring tears to the eyes of a harder man than I am, which are like a fervent appeal to be granted soul' (p. 501, LP 385). Above all he dwells on the double aspect of the chilling chorus of devilish laughter which closes the first part of the oratorio, reminding him uncomfortably of his friend's sardonic mirth over things which inspired awe in others. The passage is so painful to hear, he says, that he could hardly have brought himself to mention it, were it not for its involvement in what he calls 'music's most profound secret, which is a secret of identity' (p. 502, LP 385). For the opening passage of the second section is a children's choir with orchestral accompaniment, 'a piece of cosmic music of the spheres, icy, clear, transparent as glass, astringently dissonant, to be sure, but at the same time possessing an inaccessible, strange and unearthly loveliness of sound that fills the heart with longing devoid of hope'. And this passage has the same musical substance as the infernal laughter:

the instrumentation and rhythms have been completely changed; but in the delicately high-pitched, heart-rending angelic song there is not a single note that does not have its strict counterpart in the hellish laughter. (p. 503, LP 386)

Zeitblom glimpses here a desire to compose a very different kind of music, kept in check by the integrity of Leverkühn's vision. Adorno's account of the necessary isolation of modernist art is at work again:

Advanced music has no choice but to insist on remaining 'hard', without any concessions to those humane values whose tempting offers, wherever they are still to be found, it sees through as the mask of inhumanity. (PdnM, p. 28)

Obedience to this imperative to remain 'hard' does not come easily to Leverkühn, despite his lack of 'soul'. At a point when, Zeitblom surmises, the idea of the *Apocalipsis cum figuris* was already growing in his mind (p. 419, LP 321), Leverkühn composes a work in a very different vein, his puppet-opera on tales from the *Gesta Romanorum*, and in particular the legend of the 'holy sinner' to whom Mann was later to devote a short novel of his own. At the core of this story is Pope Gregory, a child of incest who unwittingly himself enters an incestuous marriage, all of which 'horrendous circumstances are not only no obstacle to his eventual elevation to be Vicar of Christ, but through God's miraculous grace actually make him appear particularly called and predestined to fill that office' (p. 422, LP 323). Here is a life where ostracism, transgression and marginality are so many signs of election, triumphantly vindicated as such by the final course of events. But the vindication, Leverkühn wistfully recognises in the parodistic manner of his setting and his deliberate choice of the 'intrinsically grotesque' (p. 426, LP 326) medium of puppets, is indeed a matter of legend, not a model to which he can realistically aspire. All the same, while this work is in progress, Leverkühn envisages 'the bringing together of the avant-garde with folk-art, the removal of the gulf between art and accessibility'. The appropriate means to this end could not be sentimentality or false naivety (vices of which Adorno accused all those contemporary composers who did not fit his bill of relentless inaccessibility, Stravinsky foremost among them) but 'irony, mockery which, clearing the air, would combat Romanticism, pathos, prophecy, luxuriance of sound and literariness [a sequence of attributes clearly meant to identify, above all, the theory and practice of Wagner] by enlisting as its allies objective and elemental features: that is to say, through the rediscovery of music itself as the organisation of time' (p. 427, LP 327). Leverkühn, who has apparently committed himself to a path that will take him very far away indeed from an art 'readily understandable to all', has 'a tremor in his voice' — as Zeitblom tells us twice over (pp. 429; 430, LP 328; 329) — when he predicts a future for art strikingly unlike the anguished isolation of his own life and work:

The whole atmosphere in which art exists, will, believe me, change — it will grow much more carefree and modest: that's unavoidable, and something to be glad about. It will shed a great deal of melancholy ambition and acquire a new innocence, a new innocuousness in fact. The future will see in art, and art will see in itself, the servant of a community ... which will not possess a 'culture' but may actually be one. It is hard for us to imagine, and yet it will come about and be perfectly natural: an art free of suffering, spiritually healthy, without solemnity or sadness, amicable, an art on familiar terms with humanity.

(p. 429, LP 328)

Leverkühn's rare betrayal of emotion as he evokes this future so dramatically remote from his own understanding and experience is, like the 'longing' that surfaces briefly in *Apocalipsis cum figuris*, the sign of a wish to go beyond negation, to participate in and enjoy a quality of creative existence which the contemporary world simply does not make available to him, and which he can consequently approach only by self-deception or a denial of his critical insight. It is how he could live and work if only his vision were less penetrating and his judgement less incorruptible. And it is how he likes to think others will be able to live in an age to come, where society has been (somehow) freed from alienation; but in the meantime he must remain true to the destiny which has assigned him the role of suffering witness to this alienation, called to testify to it through the bleak 'hardness' of his music. So his must be a 'longing without hope', at least as far as his personal prospects of a less fraught existence are concerned. For him, as for another modernist artist who self-consciously drew on the discourse of religious faith in the cause of fixing his creative identity amid fragmentation and rootlessness, 'hope would be hope for the wrong thing'.

Temptations to humanity

The penultimate phase in Leverkühn's life, prepared for by these passages, stands under the aspect of a belated, and essentially half-hearted, attempt to enjoy something of that existence 'on familiar terms with humanity' which, according to his deepest convictions, he cannot attain without self-betrayal. Zeitblom reveals his irritation that Leverkühn talks about his vision of a future condition of art in the presence of Rudi Schwerdtfeger who, he patronisingly comments, 'doubtless had some trouble following the conversation' (p. 427, LP 327). In Zeitblom's eyes, Schwerdtfeger epitomises all those whose stupidity allows them to partake wholeheartedly of what in Mann's Novelle

Tonio Kröger (1903) were called 'the joys of ordinariness'. It is in terms reminiscent of Mann's early fiction that Zeitblom explains Ines Rodde's (literally) fatal attraction to the violinist: 'for surely [Schwerdtfeger] represented something like the charms of life [das liebe Leben] in the eyes of her knowledge-laden melancholy' (p. 395, LP 302). 'Knowledge-laden melancholy' is something to which Adrian Leverkühn is no stranger either; and this makes it understandable that he turns to Schwerdtfeger as a partner in what he will later grotesquely call, to his face, 'a rehearsal for being human' (p. 579, LP 447).

The short-lived liaison with Schwerdtfeger begins when the composer of *Apocalipsis cum figuris*, now in his thirty-ninth year, seems more intensely and harrowingly isolated than ever before. He is surrounded by an 'atmosphere of indescribable strangeness and solitude ... which gave the impression that he came from a country where nobody else lived' (p. 545, LP 419). Zeitblom has in his possession a letter which Leverkühn wrote to Schwerdtfeger at about this time, which in its 'painful openness' reads 'like the laying bare of a wound'. This letter, which Schwerdtfeger 'naturally ought to have destroyed' (p. 552, LP 424), is the beginning of a relationship which produces what Schwerdtfeger calls 'a platonic child'(p. 467, LP 358), Leverkühn's violin concerto, and admits Schwerdtfeger to the tiny circle of those whom Leverkühn addresses with the familiar form 'du' (Zeitblom, as a former schoolfriend, is the only other member, apart from the family whom he never in any case sees). There is an obvious reminiscence here of the phrase Leverkühn used to talk of the utopian future where art would be 'on friendly terms with' (literally: 'say "du" to') humanity. Just how problematic this relationship is in terms of Leverkühn's personality and values is amply demonstrated in the concerto itself.

The violin concerto, on Zeitblom's account, 'does not fit in with the rest of Leverkühn's remorselessly radical and implacable oeuvre' (p. 542, LP 417). Its first movement, initially of uncertain key, but soon settling into a clear C major, is 'of a sweetness and tenderness kept just this side of mockery', and it employs familiar romantic techniques of virtuoso violin writing 'in a half respectful, half caricaturing way' (p. 544, LP 418). Precisely Schwerdtfeger, whose limited intellectual powers are repeatedly stressed, is allowed to make the point about how far this work, written 'with him in mind', diverges from the rest of Leverkühn's mature compositions. The occasion is the conversation, which Zeitblom concedes he could not have witnessed but nevertheless claims to be able to reproduce in every detail (p. 576, LP 444), in which Leverkühn persuades Schwerdtfeger to propose on his behalf to Marie Godeau. This proposal appears as ambivalent from its first mention in the narrative. Leverkühn will present the idea of marrying as yet another stage in the 'humanisation' of his life and his art, a further advance along the road to emotional integration which his liaison with Schwerdtfeger had begun. Well before this point, however, Zeitblom has started his account of the episode of Leverkühn's marriage plans as an act of 'revenge', aimed at removing Schwerdtfeger and all that he represents from his life. Having 'condescended' to be on familiar terms with Schwerdtfeger, Zeitblom comments as he begins section XXXIX, Leverkühn 'could not help avenging the abasement which that involved, for all the happiness it may have brought him. The vengeance was involuntary, swift, cold-hearted and mysterious' (p. 553, LP 425).

Schwerdtfeger is quick to detect that Leverkühn is protesting too much when he stresses the 'human' aspect of his wish to marry, especially when he claims that marriage would do wonders for 'the human content' of his future works.

That's four times now you've said 'human'. I've been keeping count… There's something incredibly unsuitable and, and – humiliating about [the word] coming from you. Forgive me for saying so. Was your music inhuman so far? Then in the end, it's the inhumanity that makes it great. I'm sorry if I sound stupid, but I wouldn't fancy hearing a humanly inspired work of yours.

With this remark, Schwerdtfeger has conceded that the violin concerto is a derogation from Leverkühn's characteristic 'greatness', and Leverkühn skewers him on this admission:

Wouldn't you really? Are you absolutely sure you wouldn't? Then
how come you've played such a work three times in public? And
accepted its dedication? ... Here's someone telling me that I've
nothing to do with humanity, indeed that I'm forbidden to have
anything to do with it, when it was that same someone who won me
over to humanity with astonishing patience ... someone with whom
for the first time in my life I found human warmth.

(p. 579, LP 446)

Outmanoeuvred, Schwerdtfeger consents to be the bearer of his
friend's proposal. The immediate outcome is that the harbingers
of humanity, Schwerdtfeger and Marie Godeau, are removed
from Leverkühn's life for good; and in the longer term, via a
sequence of events for which Leverkühn, backed up by some
of Zeitblom's comments as narrator, will eventually claim
responsibility, the mission leads to 'poor Rudi's' violent death
at the hands of Ines Rodde.

Leverkühn's marriage plans were ambivalent from the start.
Zeitblom, flabbergasted to learn of Adrian's interest in Marie
Godeau, is worried about the way his friend talks as if 'there
were no need to be concerned about the girl's consent' (p. 560,
LP 430). He concludes that, at some level of his awareness,
Leverkühn had anticipated being rejected all along. Yet Marie
Godeau is neither a frivolous nor a random choice. Apart from
her possession of those black eyes that signal Leverkühn's
deep-seated erotic interest − she also has his mother's facial
shape, oval with a slightly pointed chin (pp. 33; 556, LP 19;
427) − her personality and career embody a set of alternative
possibilities which Leverkühn is simultaneously acknowledging
and dismissing from his existence. These possibilities are not
merely to do with human companionship; they encompass
Marie's way of life, her close and creative involvement as a
stage designer with art, but in a mode of active interchange
and partnership with production teams, directors and play-
wrights centred on successful public performance, and so very
different from Leverkühn's rural withdrawal, her cosmopolitan
outlook, her bilingualism, the ease with which she moves
between francophone and German cultural spheres. She
represents once again that urbane 'world' in which the

impresario Fitelberg tries in vain to win Leverkühn's participation during a lightning visit to Pfeiffering, only in a much less alien and threatening form. Zeitblom understands this well enough:

> What came towards him in her person, was it not that 'world' which he so shunned in his solitude – including the 'world' understood in terms of music and art, as the specifically non-German? Came towards him in a form that was highly serious yet kindly, awakening trust, holding out the promise of bringing what he lacked, encouraging him to union? Did he not love her from out of his oratorio-world of musical theology and mathematical magic numbers?   (p. 561, LP 431)

These are plainly rhetorical questions: while evoking the attractiveness of Marie to Leverkühn, Zeitblom is simultaneously rehearsing the reasons why the promise of 'union' must be spurious. In feeling drawn to Marie and in dramatically rejecting her through the stratagem of an intentionally hopeless proposal inspired by literary models, Leverkühn is once more asserting the priorities that have made him a great artist at the conscious price of 'soul' and 'human warmth'. It is his counterpart to the re-ratification of the pact by which the *Faustbuch* figure terminates the brief flirtation with the idea of repentance instigated by his pious neighbour.

Visitation

Leverkühn's alternation between bouts of sterility accompanied by disabling illness and episodes of imperious creative energy continues into the last period of his career, a constant reminder of the devil's predictions and the pathological element in his genius. Twenty-one years after the making of the 'pact', 1927 proves to be an *annus mirabilis* for chamber composition, bringing a piece for strings, woodwind and piano, a string quartet and a string trio, all of which receive extensive and exuberant descriptions provided by the Mann-Adorno verbal composing team (pp. 605–7, LP 466–8). It is at this time that Zeitblom records an increasing habit on Leverkühn's part of speaking, as well as writing, in phrases borrowed from the linguistic sphere of the *Faustbuch* (p. 608, LP 469). The twenty-four years of 'demonic' time which Leverkühn believes he has been allotted are drawing to a close, and he is beginning to think of drawing up a balance in a work that will have his self-identification with Faust as its central theme. The arrival of his nephew Nepomuk or 'Echo' is described as an 'incident' that for the time being 'distracts' him from this project (p. 609, LP 469); but in the event it is the encounter with Echo and the impact of his death that gives Leverkühn the final impetus to compose his last masterpiece.

The figure of Echo is perhaps the most daring example of over-determination in a novel where virtually everything and everyone, thanks to the densely-woven texture of allusions, has to carry a burden of surplus meaning. He is a six-year-old staying with his uncle while his mother is convalescing; he is 'the' archetypal child; he is a benign nature-spirit like Shakespeare's Ariel; and he is a messenger from a realm beyond nature, an angel. At the least metaphysical end of this spectrum, Echo is a pre-socialised human being, not yet subject to alienation. He is 'still not at the age where a boy has to stand up and pay his respects when adults approach' (p. 616, LP 475), and he is, like the utopian art Leverkühn dreamed of, 'per du', on familiar terms, with everyone, not yet needing to observe the niceties of forms of address. He correspondingly embodies something of that imagined future atmosphere of easeful community to which Leverkühn hoped art might one day attain. As a nature-spirit, he personifies a prelapsarian world from which humanity has fallen away through its divisions and strife. In this guise, he inspires his uncle to settings of Ariel's songs from *The Tempest*. He asks his uncle how old Ariel was after his twelve years of captivity, and is told 'Ariel wasn't any age at all, before and after his bondage he was always the same graceful child of the air' (p. 624, LP 480). Zeitblom's more prosaic turn of mind tries to dwell on the fact that Echo's 'adorable charm' is nevertheless 'under the sway of time' (p. 619, LP 476), yet finds himself forced to concede that Echo's 'validity as the manifestation *par excellence* of the child on earth' is 'something that made one incapable of believing in time and its base doings, its power over this wondrous vision'. Finally, there is Echo as angel, as the 'fair messenger' who has 'descended to earth' from a lofty realm (p. 619, LP 477) and whose childish rhymes seem to contain some sort of 'message' which earthbound ears can marvel at, but not truly understand (p. 612, LP 472), as if his presence were a sign that some divine power was benevolently concerned about the plight of benighted mortals.

Zeitblom is in no doubt that Leverkühn 'dearly loved his little nephew from the very first day, and that his arrival had begun a new, delightful era in his existence' (p. 620, LP 477). This delight has more than a little to do with what Zeitblom explains as Leverkühn's characteristically artistic tendency to 'believe in the image', to 'lend to inexorable change the aspect of timeless being' (p. 619, LP 477). The tendency of precisely the Nietzschean artist, burdened with disabling knowledge, to come to believe in the reality of what is, in the end, only an image of beauty, was a phenomenon whose destructive consequences Mann had long ago explored in *Death in Venice*. Here, the torment and death of Echo before his very eyes is all the more harrowing to Leverkühn precisely because he had, for all his customary 'cold' scepticism, come to 'believe' in Echo as a manifestation of something that relativised his otherwise relentlessly bleak vision.

The way Echo dies is a mockery of all the values and ideals his existence seemed to embody. His succumbing to an infectious illness belies the arcadian image of a nature peopled by benign spirits and emphasises the brutality precisely of natural processes when judged by human standards of good and evil. The celebrated specialist called in to give a second opinion, with his overriding concern to 'see a correct and clear progression of the case though all its stages' (p. 631, LP 487), highlights the sense in which what is happening is, for all the relative rarity of this particular kind of meningitis, a perfectly normal sequence of events within a natural order where feelings count for nothing. The swiftness of Echo's passage from radiant well-being to agony and death shows that he is in fact mercilessly subject to time and change. And the affront this offers to morality and justice means that, in the end, Echo's 'angelic' function is effectively reversed. Once an apparent harbinger of a divine realm of joy and light breaking into the world of mankind, he becomes in his suffering evidence of powers of malevolent evil wreaking wanton destruction. To do justice to his sense of outrage at this spectacle of 'incomprehensible cruelty', Zeitblom himself resorts to language suggesting diabolical intervention, saying that Echo was 'swept away with horrendous savagery and fury' (p. 627, LP 484), and Leverkühn, reminded all the more forcibly by this dramatic lesson in transitoriness that his allotted span is drawing to a close, sees the devil's signature in the same 'pitiful resources' (p. 632, LP 488) of pathological destruction with which he himself has entered into complicity in the interests of his art.

There are only two junctures in Leverkühn's life, at opposite ends of his creative span, when he is not to some degree under the 'cooling' influence of his critical intellect. The first is his compulsion to seek out 'Esmeralda', when the power of 'soulless drives' (p. 198, LP 150) gains the upper hand. The second comes in the intensity of anguish with which Echo's death fills him, an access of overwhelming emotion unchecked by any analytical reservation, of the kind which the devil had declared him incapable, in a passage of their dialogue which will have an important part to play in the examination of Leverkühn's putative 'salvation'. The first of these events is the origin, not only of his syphilitic infection, but of the notion of serial composition. The second precipitates him into the creation of his last work which is at one and the same time a repudiation of his chosen path and its anguished vindication.

Expression reconstructed

Leverkühn provides a formula for the import of his last work, *The Lamentation of Dr Faustus*, while Echo is still on his deathbed: he intends to 'revoke' Beethoven's Ninth Symphony. This 'revocation' is plainly meant to be much more than a musical statement. What Leverkühn is withdrawing, declaring null and void through his 'Ode to Grief', is a whole complex of beliefs and aspirations enshrined in Beethoven's composition and Schiller's *Ode to Joy* which provides the text of its final movement. He is proposing to give musical embodiment to a fundamentally different set of beliefs about the relationship between humane values and the possibility of their realisation in any available world. He has come to the conclusion that 'It is not to be ... the Good and the Noble, what people call the humane' (p. 634, LP 489), and this conviction forms one component in the 'lament' which his last work expresses, 'the most horrendous human and divine lamentation that has ever been intoned on earth, starting from the individual self, but then spreading out further and further until it engulfs as it were the entire cosmos' (p. 643, LP 497). The lament is essentially about cosmic solitude as the condition of humanity. The 'starting point' from which the lament grows outwards is Leverkühn's ambivalent final judgement upon his 'destiny': on the one hand, his conviction of the necessity of his musical development as the sole adequate response to the truth of his perceptions; on the other hand, his outrage at a world where truthfulness exacts such a price. The musical backbone of the composition is a note-row first enunciated in the setting of Faust's words (twelve syllables in German) 'For I die as a good and a bad Christian' (p. 646, LP 500). The theological significance of these words will be explored later; what matters at the moment is that they imply Leverkühn's simultaneous affirmation and repudiation of his own life and art as 'good' because demanded by integrity and 'evil' because intolerable in its cost. We are told that the twelve notes to which this utterance is set are the basis of the entire work, an hour and a quarter long. Every part of it, in melody and harmony, is strictly derived from this series, so that Leverkühn's idea of 'rigorous composition' with 'not a single free note left' (p. 646, LP 500) without resort to external tonal conventions is fully realised. Leverkühn has thus triumphantly solved the problem of constructing a 'work' without implying false claims that the external world offered something other than chaos and meaninglessness. Indeed, the cantata, in its formal and structural autonomy, castigates the external world for not offering any model of order or value worthy of affirmation. The self-contained, esoteric modernist work becomes, through the sheer intensity of its self-generated rigour, a ferocious indictment of a universe devoid of intrinsic worth and order. This seems to be at the root of Zeitblom's claims that 'this, [Leverkühn's] most rigorous work, a work with the most extreme degree of calculation, is at the same time purely expressive' (p. 647, LP 500). Leverkühn has finally achieved the 'breakthrough' to pure expression that he has long dreamed of. For the first and last time in his creative life, he writes a piece entirely devoid of parody, even though it draws on a vast repertoire of musical devices used to express intense emotion from Monteverdi onwards:

> not as mechanical imitation ... but in as it were an admittedly conscious disposition over each and every expressive device that has ever been produced in the history of music, all of which are here, in a kind of alchemical distillation process, purified and crystallised out.
>
> (pp. 647–8, LP 501)

It is easier to see what Zeitblom is being made to assert here than it is to imagine how Leverkühn is supposed to have accomplished it. Mann's working notes reveal that his original idea was to have the *Lamentation* remain a fragment, unfinished at the moment of Leverkühn's collapse (and maybe even triggering that collapse by the sheer irresolvability of the task it presented). It was Adorno who persuaded him to make Leverkühn's final work the achieved culmination of his career, whilst remaining very much in the domain of bleak 'negativity'. The claim is that through the composer's 'conscious' and yet not 'mechanical' dispositions, a panoply of expressive means drawn from four centuries of music is purged of their historical connections and associations so that they are not so much (parodistically) reused as deployed for the first time in their true 'crystallised' essence, which is said to be nothing other than universal lament at mankind's cosmic isolation. Leverkühn's crowning achievement is to extract the innermost meaning of the entire Western musical tradition, express that meaning with unsurpassable clarity and intensity, and by so doing bring the tradition to an end in a work of 'truly extreme historical finality' (p. 640, LP 495). His early anxieties about a commitment to composition centred on his fear that there would be nothing for him to say in a voice of his own. Now, at the end of his career, he is able to create a work that is uniquely his own in both structure and content, and yet is also a 'résumé' (p. 647, LP 500) of the music – and not just the music – of an entire historical epoch. After this, there really is nothing for anyone else to say within the tradition he is bringing to a close as first the choir 'loses itself' in the final orchestral movement, then, group by group, the instruments fall silent, until 'the last word', a high G on a solo cello, 'slowly fades away' so that 'nothing remains, – silence and night'(p. 651, LP 503). Having written Western music out of existence, there is little left for Leverkühn to do but summon an assembly analogous to the audience of Faust's parting speeches, introduce the cantata as the final fruit of a diabolical pact, and then collapse into the obliviousness of incurable insanity. The life and the art have, in the end, consumed each other.

Chapter 3

Matters theological

Parody and transcendence

In the last years of his life, Thomas Mann increasingly thought of himself as a 'religious' author. Two concepts recur in conjunction with this idea. The first is 'reverence [Ehrfurcht] towards the mystery that is man' (IX, 711). The second, frequently encountered in *Doctor Faustus*, is association of religion with paradox. The two ideas are linked, since Mann views paradox as the site of mystery and consequently as a stimulus to reverence. Where reason encounters things which require the application of contradictory concepts or judgements, there is an inkling of a reality which human categories cannot master, an intimation of transcendence. This outlook is, however, difficult to reconcile with a way of thinking schooled by Nietzsche's militant and programmatic immanence, where mystery is relentlessly unmasked as mystification in the interests of some will to power, and paradox is dissolved into the inevitable differences between distinct perspectives on a constantly changing flux.

All the same, Mann was clearly determined to make his novel a religious work in more than an incidental sense. Any novel on the Faust theme will use concepts drawn from the language of religious belief, but the more those concepts are redefined in terms of an author's own vision, the less they guarantee a religious dimension in the finished work. Thomas Mann, like Goethe before him, engages in substantial and comprehensive secular redefinition of most of the key concepts in the Faust story; but unlike Goethe, he seems unhappy about his own secularism. He attempts to restore to the experiences of Zeitblom and Leverkühn some of the religious dimension which his analogical use of theological notions has removed.

The most obvious instance is the extremely odd idea of making Leverkühn both a reincarnation of Nietzsche *and* a strongly religious 'Lutheran'. It is striking that both the first 'revelation' of Leverkühn's religious disposition (see above, p. 23) and one of its last manifestations in his final address (see below, p. 79) rely on misquotations from scripture which must be laid at Mann's door, rather than his character's. The alleged quotation from Romans XIII, 'That which is of God is ordered', came to Mann via the distorting lens of the *Malleus Maleficarum*, the inquisitorial manual for witch-hunters which he used for much of his material on necromancy and its detection. And, as we shall see, the other would-be Pauline text on which Leverkühn pins many of his hopes of 'salvation' has an even shakier basis. Such slips are signs of a determination to force links that refuse to arise from the material to hand. The same strain can be seen in the motivation, if such it can be called, of Leverkühn's initial choice to study theology. At the most superficial level, this is a constraint imposed by the *Faustbuch* model, whose central character started off as a theologian, but that need hardly have been binding. After all, if Faust's main preoccupation, ritual magic, can be replaced by musical composition, there is no good reason why his initial interest should not have been similarly transposed, especially since Mann had given Leverkühn a strong interest in mathematics. A Leverkühn who put aside Einsteinian pursuit of divine subtlety through differential equations in order to take up musical 'numerical magic' would have been no worse an image of Faustian apostasy, and more in keeping with the temperament and psychology ascribed to Leverkühn than a theologian manqué. The constraint to make Leverkühn start from theology plainly went deeper. It has to do with the determination to assert a more than analogical link between Leverkühn's destiny and a story of sin and damnation, and the need to weave into the novel's texture various threads that strengthen that link. The ideas introduced via theological lectures by Ehrenfried Kumpf and Eberhard Schleppfuß can be passed off as samples of what went on in theological faculties in the late nineteenth century, whereas fictitious lectures on mathematics would have presented more of a problem. Through Kumpf, a liberal theologian who nevertheless throws things at the devil in *imitatio Lutheri*, the crucial notion of an unfrivolous parody of Lutheran discourse as a way of expressing a modern religious sensibility is introduced; and through Schleppfuß we enter thickets of ambivalence where the paths of depth psychology, moral theology and sheer humbug can elaborately cross.

The borrowing of Lutheran language and gesture, patterned on Kumpf, reveals its full power in Leverkühn's narrative of his first visit to the brothel and Zeitblom's commentary on it, a section of the text which provides a paradigm for the role of parody in the entire novel. Introducing what follows as an account of 'what is afoot between me and Satan' (p. 189, LP 142), his first reference to personal dealings with the devil, Leverkühn tells the episode in the mock-sixteenth-century diction he will later affect to introduce his record of the conversation with the devil and to address the gathering he calls together to hear his final address. Zeitblom offers an explanation for this strange linguistic manner in a passage which is of decisive significance for the role of parody in this novel:

Let me just say first, that the old-fashioned language is naturally intended as parody and is an allusion ... to the characteristic speech of Ehrenfried Kumpf, – but at the same time it is an expression of personality, a piece of self-stylisation, a manifestation of a unique inner form and inclination, which uses parody in a highly distinctive way, both hides and fulfils itself under its guise.

(pp. 185–6, LP 139)

And these remarks are taken up after the letter has been cited, as Zeitblom speculates that the verbal manner was chosen to give the incident its due 'religious atmosphere', and to allow Leverkühn to conclude his account by saying 'And so amen, and pray for me!' This phrase in particular commands Zeitblom's attention in his reflections on the import of the parodistic style:

How else, without this play [with language], could those words have been written, which needed to be written nonetheless: 'Pray for me!'? There can be no better example of quotation as facade, parody as pretext.

(p. 194, LP 147)

Here parody appears in a rather different light than it does when the devil refers to it as 'aristocratic nihilism' (p. 322, LP 246), a symptom of having nothing substantial to say and merely manipulating the empty shell of what were once significant devices. This is parody chosen as the uniquely appropriate expressive medium for a particular task. Leverkühn is trying to convey as truthful an account as he can of what is superficially a trivial event, but which he and Zeitblom know is a psychological trauma likely to have far-reaching consequences. The truthfulness involves conveying both the ribald surface and the dangerous undertones of the encounter; and it also requires Leverkühn to express his own complex attitude to what has happened and what it meant to him, an attitude compounded of seriousness and self-mockery. Precisely this complex truthfulness is achieved through the stylised narration. Moreover, the borrowed discourse allows Leverkühn to make an appeal to his friend for which there is simply no available concept in his everyday language. Apart from the last words of the novel, prayer does not appear to be an activity for which Zeitblom, for all his ostensible Catholicism, has much use. Nor does Leverkühn show any sign, when talking in his own voice, of a belief in the power of prayer in any orthodox sense. All the same, the idea of prayer has been raised in connection with Leverkühn's theological studies, where Zeitblom reports him as saying:

I think I understand what Aristotle meant by entelechy. It's the individual's angel, the tutelary spirit of his life, in whose wise guidance he is glad to trust. What people call prayer is really a declaration of this trust, either in apprehension or in supplication.

(pp. 127–8, LP 94)

The injunction to Zeitblom to 'pray for' him is consequently not just a linguistic flourish that belongs merely to the surface of the parodistic writing: it is an expression of Leverkühn's sense that he is relating a decisive moment in his personal destiny and that he wants Zeitblom to share his feeling of existential exposure.

In other words, parody is not here a sign of creative sterility, but an enabling device that conveys events and attitudes with a precision and subtlety that a less indirect style could not achieve. Though disparaged by characters within the text, especially through its associations with the less demanding and ambitious of Leverkühn's compositions, parody is exemplified and embodied in the novel overall, just as in Leverkühn's letter, as the narrative manner appropriate to a comprehensive and internalised perspectivism: that is, a perspectivism that does not simply set the viewpoints of various individuals one alongside the other, but which renders the consciousness of a subject of experience who is 'modest' in Nietzsche's sense (see above p. A-10), whose own repertoire of categories and values is permeated by an awareness of their historical relativity. For it is historical relativism that is at stake in Mann's refinement of parody as an expressive device. Parody of the kind that is decried within the novel as sterile relies on a confident belief that what is outdated can be clearly identified and safely if affectionately mocked (hence 'aristocratic nihilism'). The parody practised through the novel's array of devices is, by contrast, informed by a constant awareness of the precariousness of the standpoint from which the judgement of 'outdatedness' is made. This 'modesty' is the opposite of an 'aristocratic' position; and because the oscillation between the ample discourse of the past and the hesitant tones of the present weaves a linguistic mesh in which, for all its fragility, values are held long enough to be glimpsed, if not quite scrutinised, it is anything but 'nihilistic'.

This technique bears not only upon judgements of value made by characters, but also upon their judgements about what is and is not real, the most striking example, over which critics have tirelessly and fruitlessly laboured, being Leverkühn's encounter with the devil. Mann here follows Dostoyevsky closely in making the objective reality of the visitor very much an issue within the dialogue, though in such a way that the question is clouded rather than resolved. In both novels, pathology is said to be at work. Ivan's apparition, we are told by Dostoyevsky's narrator, was the first indication of what later developed into insanity; Leverkühn and his visitor both agree that their encounter is a sign that the infection contracted some five years previously has now reached a decisive stage.

But the devil claims that the progress of the disease is only the occasion, not the cause, of what Leverkühn sees, 'enabling' him to perceive (by which we can understand something like: give symbolic form to) a power of evil that was in any case there (p. 313, LP 239). The possibility that Leverkühn's recorded dialogue does reflect an encounter with something or someone outside his own person, that the devil may be *in* his mind without being wholly and purely *of* his mind, is just about left open.

Here the affinity, but also the distance between paradox and parody as windows upon the transcendent becomes visible. Paradox claims to fix the trace of transcendence by a harsh and firmly defined clash between contradictory notions, whereas deeply serious parody of religious language and notions of the kind employed in the novel hints at the possibility of transcendence by an exhaustive and constantly shifting play of possibilities in which everything that can count against the existence of a domain beyond human understanding is brought into interaction with a discourse rooted in an age where such a domain was part of the conceptual repertoire of an entire culture. Leverkühn himself, like Ivan Karamazov, is left uncertain as to whether he really has met the devil (an uncertainty which in both novels is distinct from the character's doubts about whether he was dreaming); but the significance of the encounter, bodied forth through parodistic language, has the full impact of a living and waking experience. Beyond that assertion, the novel does not allow us to go; but nor does it provide any authority for stopping short of it at a confidently reductionist position.

Sin as redemption, despair as hope

There is in fact not much by way of compelling paradox in the novel, though Mann probably thought otherwise. Two main areas are offered as instances of paradox with strong religious implications. The first is the 'dialectical' relationship between good and evil, so that the great sin is somehow an instrument of sanctity: the second is the idea of an intense kinship between despair and hope, so that the right to hope is granted to those who achieve the bleakest degree of despair. Both these notions (along with the idea that their incorporation into the text will give the work a strong 'religious' aura) are heavily dependent on a particular reading of Dostoyevsky, with the second notion also being fostered by Mann's belated acquaintance with Kierkegaard's ideas.

The essence of this reading is contained in Mann's reference, on more than one occasion, to 'Dostoyevsky's profound, criminal, saintly countenance' (IX, 656 et passim). This points to a preoccupation with a certain type of Dostoyevskian character, together with a naive assignment of the traits of this character to the author. Dostoyevsky himself, then, is 'profound', 'criminal' and 'saintly', not by turns, but at one and the same time; and this combination is what makes him a preeminently religious author in Mann's eyes. In this light, Zeitblom's response of 'religious awe' at the thought of Leverkühn's deliberate self-infection (see above, p. 37) acquires yet another dimension. The deliberate contraction of a fatal disease by consorting with a prostitute is meant as a Dostoyevskian deed of spectacular sinfulness, of desperate yet heroic self-abandonment which bears in itself the seeds of salvation through the radical commitment to extreme risk which it represents. The hold of this mystique of sin over Thomas Mann's imagination was very strong throughout his career (it was echoed, though less strenuously, by a writer otherwise as unlike Mann as could be imagined, in Heinrich Böll's pervasive assumption that scruffiness is next to godliness).

The idea that despair is the purest form of hope is expounded with great emphasis by Zeitblom in his description of *The Lamentation of Dr Faustus*, where he detects

a negative portrayal of the religious domain [eine Negativität des Religiösen], by which I certainly do not mean its denial. A work that is concerned with the tempter, with the fall from grace, with damnation, what else could it be other than a religious work!

(pp. 649–50, LP 502)

This is another version of the idea that the great sinner is closer to the saint than what Leverkühn, in his parting address, calls 'tolerably and moderately sinful people' (p. 658, LP 509), and Zeitblom uses it to prepare for his final claim about the *Lamentation* in particular, and about Leverkühn's life and work in general: that it has been so arduously insistent in its denial of any hope or possibility of comfort that it 'corresponds to' what Zeitblom calls

the religious paradox ... that in the profoundest dereliction [Heillosig-keit] lie, if only as the faintest of suggestions, the seeds of hope. That would be hope beyond hopelessness, the transcendence of despair – not its betrayal, but the miracle that surpasses faith.

(p. 651, LP 503)

This is Zeitblom, and beyond him Thomas Mann, at his most vacuously rhetorical. The puzzling final phrase (a miracle may reward or confirm faith, but how could it 'surpass' it?) is only the finishing touch in the creation of a mood of high 'religious' solemnity which relies rather too heavily on the reader's readiness to honour cheques drawn on a deposit of faith to which Thomas Mann has made no contributions. Sin as a portal to salvation, despair as the precondition of faith (rather than hope), these have a clear significance in the respective theological worlds of Dostoyevsky and Kierkegaard, but here they are used at some distance from any metaphysical underpinning.

Leverkühn as 'murderer'

The choice of Faust as paradigm keeps the issue of Leverkühn's salvation or damnation in the forefront of attention. It is hard to avoid the impression that on this question, novelist and reader are often at cross purposes. Many of the devices Mann musters seem to presuppose that it is a supremely difficult task to exculpate Leverkühn, to grant him any hint of salvation, in whatever sense, without the reader feeling that he has been let off too lightly. In fact, the problem is rather the reverse. Most readers find it hard to see why Leverkühn should be in danger of damnation, analogical or literal, in the first place. Leaving aside for the moment the problematic area of his supposed complicity in the death of Schwerdtfeger, Leverkühn does no harm to anyone but himself, and seems to be on the whole considerate and inoffensive in his dealings with others. We keep being told by Zeitblom, and by Leverkühn himself, that he is 'arrogant' and 'proud', but we search in vain for anything more offensive than a sober recognition (even slightly shamefaced at times) of his own incontestable intellectual and creative gifts. He is tactful in his expressions of dissent, far from overweening in presenting his ideas, and if he harbours contempt towards others, he keeps it well concealed. There is a notable contrast here, not just with the biographies of the real-life composers – a cantankerous and vain bunch on the whole – which Mann studied in his preparations for the novel, but with the life of Nietzsche, to whom the epithets 'arrogant' and 'proud', so tenuously affixed to Leverkühn, adhere much more firmly. Especially noticeable is Leverkühn's complete lack of the haughty and often petulant expectation of disciplehood by which Nietzsche overtaxed and ruined friendships. Not least among Leverkühn's endearing traits is his inexhaustible tolerance of the bumbling windbag who has decided, quite unbidden, to make him the centre of his life. One wonders whether Mann's greatest despiser, Vladimir Nabokov, was not intending a travesty of the relationship between Zeitblom and Leverkühn in his portrayal of that other self-appointed and voluble custodian of a creative legacy, Charles Kinbote, who proves in the end to have been significant to his deceased 'friend' only as the putative employer of 'some neighbour's gardener' in line 998 of John Shade's thousand-line poem *Pale Fire*.

We shall see how Mann tries to give Leverkühn a kind of guilt by analogy from which he can then perhaps be redeemed, but he seems to have recognised that something more substantial and immediate was needed to underwrite his potential damnation. That something is the motif which culminates in Leverkühn's final address when he tells his bemused audience 'I sit here before you as a murderer' (p. 664, LP 513), having allegedly 'sent [Schwerdtfeger] to his death'. This self-accusation has been long and carefully prepared. Zeitblom introduces the episode which ends with Schwerdtfeger's shooting as a tale of 'cold-hearted, mysterious [revenge]'. The word 'mysterious' alerts us to another attempt to draw on Dostoyevsky's authority as a source of 'religious' motifs. In an essay written during his work on *Doctor Faustus*, Mann speaks of Dostoyevsky's 'ability to suggest mysterious *guilt* and to make it form the background of the existence of his ... creations' (IX, 661), and sets up the ability to do this as a measure of artistic profundity, contrasted rather snidely with the 'psychological novelties, shock effects and fripperies' deployed by Proust (IX, 659). Premeditated murder does not otherwise figure in Mann's fiction. The death of the magician Cipolla at the hands of Mario is, like the actual shooting of Schwerdtfeger in the tramcar, very much a *crime passionnel*. But Mann seems to have wanted to enhance Leverkühn's guilt by implicating him in a Dostoyevskian death through malice aforethought, blending the motif of the planned murder with Father Zossima's doctrine of universal moral responsibility of each for all (which would allow Leverkühn to assume guilt for Echo's death as well). Leverkühn, manoeuvring Schwerdtfeger into the position that will eventually bring him before Ines Institoris's gun-barrel, is presumably meant to be a more conscious and calculating counterpart to Ivan Karamazov in the fateful conversation with Smerdyakov that leads to their father's violent end. And when Leverkühn declares himself guilty of Echo's death, on no more substantial a basis than the similarity between the syphilitic bacteria which he has knowingly released into his own central nervous system and the meningitis organisms which killed his nephew, he is here too being brought (or rather, forced) into a context of co-responsibility for evil such as Dostoyevsky frequently explores.

These efforts to inculpate Leverkühn remain unimpressive, even though (or rather, precisely because) they are a device necessary to make him sufficiently evil to be in peril of damnation. What in Dostoyevsky are complex webs of responsibility uncovered through the promptings of conscience are transposed by Mann into neurotic self-denigrations testifying at best to 'guilt-feelings' rather than to anything that moral theology could recognise as genuine guilt. The psychology and philosophy of guilt embodied in Dostoyevsky's novels are rooted in the Christian doctrine of Incarnation: they make sense only to a reader who understands (without necessarily believing) the tenet that God became man and died for the sins of all, thus creating a solidarity in guilt and redemption encompassing all human beings. Outside that context, where Mann's fiction is located, such 'mysterious' guilt remains mere mystification.

Figures of salvation

For the *Faustbuch* author, the devil's disciple was unequivocally damned. For Goethe he needed, as the bearer of distinctively human aspirations, to be finally saved. Thomas Mann, in his highly self-conscious engagement with the traditional material, tries to intensify the threat of damnation to the highest possible pitch and to reduce the hope of salvation to the faintest glimmer, without, however, eliminating it. Before looking at the senses in which the possibility of Leverkühn's salvation is held out, we need to complete the survey of why he is said to merit damnation. Two of the grounds for damnation, his 'pride' and his self-imputed responsibility for the deaths of Schwerdtfeger and Echo, have already been found wanting. The other grounds lie in the symbolic significance of the components that allow him to 'break through' the creative impasse. By knowingly contracting syphilis in the cause of freeing himself from intellectual inhibitions, Leverkühn is abandoning himself to an influence which will eventually destroy everything that makes him a rational being. And in setting up the arbitrary note-row and submitting himself to its absolute dominance, he is cutting himself off from a repertoire of shared significances embodied in the tonal system, yielding up his own freedom of choice to a system which stands in no essential relationship to any personal values. We have seen that his absence of 'soul' was identified as his lack of any integrated selfhood between the extremes of impersonal drives and abstract intellect. His deliberate self-infection and his serialism are a renunciation of that middle ground between mind and senses where all European humanisms have located the specifically human domain. This makes them an analogy of a pact with the powers of evil, understood as everything that is opposed to humane civilisation.

It is from this mixture of grounds for damnation that Leverkühn has tentatively to be saved. His 'salvation' is intimated in three senses. First, he is 'saved' from 'soullessness' by the sheer intensity of his grief and rage at Echo's death. This is prepared for in the conversation with the devil, where Leverkühn raises the possibility of salvation via fear of the consequences of his pact, only to be admonished by the devil that this notion of *attritio* is 'theologically outdated': forgiveness can be granted only to those who achieve *contritio*, an absolute repudiation of evil not based on any fear of retribution, which is something the devil is confident someone as persistently reflective and ironic as Leverkühn will never be able to achieve. 'Where would a man like you find the simplicity, the spontaneous abandonment to despair, that would be the precondition of this hopeless path to salvation?' (p. 330, LP 252). The suggestion is that Leverkühn does indeed find such 'simplicity' of response as he witnesses the child's agony. Secondly, Leverkühn's truthfulness to his sense of self is equated with salvation. Here a further meaning attached to 'soul' comes into play, the Aristotelian entelechy, 'the soul of a being which impels it to self-realisation, self-perfection in the phenomenal world' (p. 127, LP 94). To be 'saved' in this sense means living out one's personal destiny to the end. In this strand of meaning, salvation lies precisely in refusing to recant, in rejecting, as does the Faust figure in Leverkühn's oratorio, the pious neighbour's exhortations to repentance as a temptation (p. 650, LP 503). The ambivalence of Leverkühn's last work, which laments the 'pact' while reaffirming it, is consequently an attempt to merit both kinds of, apparently contradictory, salvation. It provides a characteristically new sense for the quotation from the *Faustbuch*, 'I die as a good and a bad Christian' whose setting, as we have seen (above, p. 64), furnishes the note-row for the *Lamentation*. These two strands are combined and extended by the third sense in which the possibility of 'salvation' is held out, identified in the hope which Leverkühn himself expresses at the very end of his final address:

> But for all I was a sinner, my friends, a murderer, an enemy of mankind, a slave to devilish fornication, yet have I always laboured earnestly as a man of works and neither reposed ... nor slept, but toiled in the sweat of my brow and accomplished hard things, according to the words of the Apostle: 'Whoso seeketh hard things, unto him shall hardship come.' (pp. 664–5, LP 514)

The source and implications of this last piece of scriptural misquotation have been tracked down by J. P. Stern. Thomas Mann wrongly thought this text, which he found cited in a volume of Luther's letters, was from St Paul; but his most significant mistake, passed on to Leverkühn, was his notion of what it meant. Far from saying that prodigious effort is somehow 'redeeming' simply because it is strenuous, Luther is citing scripture (Proverbs XXV, 27) to warn against making life more difficult than it need be. On such shaky theological grounds does the author found Leverkühn's hope that the degree of effort and pain his chosen path has brought to him is of itself redemptive. For this reason, the attempts to give Leverkühn not only a promise of redemption but even the aura of a redeemer through aligning his sufferings in the cause of his 'works' with those of Christ are equally ill-founded and unconvincing. Mann had actually tried this, grotesquely enough, with Goethe's Faust, probably the least Christ-like figure in the whole of Western literature, ascribing to Goethe's hero the wish 'to be the Son of Man, to ... take all the suffering and joy of mankind upon himself as representative and victim' (IX, 619). Here he lets Zeitblom discern 'something Christ-like' about his friend's face (p. 640, LP 495), gives Leverkühn three attendant women in his tribulations, and has 'mother' Schweigestill, at the moment of his final collapse, cradle him in a *pietà*-like posture (p. 667, LP 516). Leverkühn himself makes the identification in a characteristically sombre way in his final oratorio, where Faust's last instruction to his students to retire to their beds and sleep soundly while he waits for the devil to fetch him is presented as 'a conscious and intentional reversal' (p. 650, LP 502) of Christ's injunction to his disciples in Gethsemane, 'tarry ye here and watch'. This is a 'religious' allusion only in the loosest sense, since it emphasises the distance rather than any affinity between Mann's solitary hero and the Christ of the Gospels. For Leverkühn-Faust as for Vigny and Rilke, both of whom wrote notable poems on the Gethsemane theme, the figure in the garden is an emblem of despair who can redeem no one by his sufferings, because he lacks that divine nature which would lend his individual agony transcendent significance and effect.

In one respect, the dubiousness of the novel's claims to a religious dimension are to its overall benefit. The trickiest problem Mann had to solve in fitting together all the strands in this immensely elaborate work was how to make Leverkühn's destiny elucidate modern German history without implying, or being taken to imply, that Germany's 'pact' with National Socialism had 'redeeming' features akin to those detected in the composer's life. Had the theological elements been more plausible, the danger of confusing the historical reckoning would have been that much greater.

Chapter 4

Germans

Realism versus allegory

The relationship between Mann's novel and the history of Germany is in one sense simple to the point of crudity. Adrian Leverkühn is meant as an allegory of modern Germany. Just as Leverkühn 'broke through' creative sterility by recourse to the 'demonic' means of syphilitic infection, so Germany tried to 'break through' the restrictions of liberal institutions and international law by an appeal to myth and instinct as energising forces. And just as Leverkühn turned to the abstract, impersonal discipline of mathematical relationships in order to give his works an order that owed nothing to Romantic conventions, so too Germany contained the potentially anarchic forces of bloodlust by a despotic political order and a reign of internal terror which had no truck with the Rights of Man. In the end, Leverkühn comes to grief as a result of his chosen priorities, and so did Germany.

These notions are unlikely to impress anyone looking for historical explanations, and they raise a serious problem. In the later stages of Leverkühn's career, his 'pact' issues into artistic masterpieces of the highest quality and significance, and his collapse is set about with intimations of 'salvation'. This might be taken allegorically to mean that something that could without obscenity be said to be good came out of Germany's 'pact' with dark forces, and that Germany's striving to 'break through' limits beyond which lie crimes against humanity deserved some kind of acknowledgement as an heroic venture. The only defences against such an interpretation are either to deny the allegorical intent (which means reading the novel resolutely against the grain) or to emphasise the failure of the global allegory.

That failure is already entailed by Mann's decision to make Leverkühn such an essentially harmless character. There may

indeed be analogies between the means Leverkühn chooses
and the practices of National Socialism; but the ends he has
in view and the way he pursues them, the genuinely costly
strenuousness of his task and the integrity with which he lives
out his hard-won vision, all bear no relation whatever to the
self-serving criminal goals and practices of Hitler's party and
state. But allegory where the detailed working-out of the
vehicle (Leverkühn's life) actually goes against an adequate
rendering of the tenor (German history) is quite simply bad
allegory. What transforms allegorical failure into narrative
success is precisely the extent to which the elaboration of
Leverkühn's life (and the lives of those associated with him) as
a citizen of twentieth-century Germany elucidates historical
forces and circumstances in the non-allegorical fashion
characteristic of European realism at its finest: by imaginatively
recreating human beings whose very individuality lays bare the
historical, social and cultural substance of their age. It is not
as an allegory of Germany but quite simply as a represented
German that Leverkühn can offer us historical insights; and
the same holds good for his partner in 'secret' identity, Serenus
Zeitblom, along with all the other figures whom the latter's
account brings before us.

National psychology

Leverkühn, Zeitblom, and the rest are 'representative' Germans
in a further sense, beyond the significance they bear as in-
habitants of their time and place embodied in a realist fiction:
they are also claimed to reveal, as individuals and in their
interaction, particular features of the German 'Volk'. The idea
of 'national character' must be treated with caution: it can be
a useful descriptive shorthand for attitudes and values which
predominate in one culture rather than another, but it has no
more explanatory force than a medical 'diagnosis' that merely
summarises symptoms. In the terms within which Thomas
Mann is operating, however, certain kinds of description of
characteristic national traits are pressed into service as the
nearest the novel gets to 'explaining' why fascism flourished

so dramatically and pervasively in Germany (for the question
of why fascism itself arose anywhere at all, the novel offers
an explanation of a different kind, which does not appeal to
particular national proclivities).

The German 'Volk' are described by Zeitblom as 'a kind of
people rather too fond of living on theory' (p. 638, LP 494);
and certainly, an excessive affection for things other than the
practical, the immediate and the given, for mental abstractions
over concrete perceptions, can be perceived in biographer and
subject alike. This trait is especially visible in the account of
conversations in the late summer of 1914, when Zeitblom was
full of the euphoria of war, seen not as a bloody and wretched
expense of life, but a symbolic regeneration and expansion of
national consciousness, and Leverkühn was under the spell
of Kleist's essay on the marionette-theatre, which was part of
the inspiration behind his vision of a future art 'on familiar
terms with humanity' (see above, p. 56). The key word that
binds their enthusiasms together is 'breakthrough' (Durch-
bruch), a notion that evokes the excitement of cutting a
Gordian knot, suddenly and dramatically bursting into a
radically new order of being without the attrition of gradual
change. In Kleist's essay, fullness of being is available only at
two extremities of an imagined spectrum of existence: the god
who knows everything and the marionette absolutely devoid of
all consciousness. Any creature possessing finite awareness,
that is, anyone we could recognise as a human person, is exiled
in the wasteland of fragmentation, insecurity and error between
these two ideal extremes, from which release can come only
through a millennial transformation such as no mundane
measures can provide. Devaluing the given and the feasible in
the cause of a theoretical construction tinged with apocalyptic
promise is the essence of the cult of 'breakthrough' which
Zeitblom and his friend, as representative Germans, share.

Visible here in the mode of hope, the same trait also
manifests itself in the cult of grandiose despair, the choice of
all-consuming catastrophe, *Götterdämmerung*, over prosaic
survival. Zeitblom detects this at work in the mentality of the
German people as well as in their fanatical leaders. Reporting

the overthrow of Mussolini, he ponders the unlikelihood of
Hitler meeting a similar fate at the hands of his own country-
men once Allied armies reach German soil:

> we watched with a mixture of horror and envy, with a powerful sense
> that we would not be capable ... of anything like it, as a country
> whose mentality allowed it to draw the sober and normal conclusion
> from a spate of scandalous defeats and losses, rid itself of its Great
> Man, and a little later agreed to what is demanded of us, too, but
> which we will never accept, so precious and sacred in our sight are
> the utmost anguish and misery: unconditional surrender. Indeed, we
> are a people quite different from all others, scornful of everything
> sober and normal, with a mightily tragic soul.   (p. 232, LP 176–7)

Zeitblom's use of 'we' throughout this passage is highly significant. On the one hand, he has as clear a perception as one could
wish of the self-destructive folly of the cult of catastrophe; on
the other hand, he feels within his own personality the pull of
the mentality he describes and has in all honesty to associate
himself with the attitudes which one part of him decries.

Zeitblom as critical observer who is nonetheless almost
mesmerised by what he observes (both in his friend and in his
nation) is a reincarnation of that bemused paterfamilias, the
narrator of *Mario and the Magician*, who sees early on in the
performance that it is 'not something for the children', but
nevertheless remains with his wife and his restless brood
through to the demeaning climax of the evening and its violent
end. Observing the inability of people of all walks of life and
intellectual ability to oppose the hypnotist's domination, that
narrator reflected that the mere will not to do something was
insufficient to withstand an intense contrary positive suggestion,
thus encapsulating the dilemma of the woolly liberal faced with
totalitarian single-mindedness. Zeitblom can be very woolly
indeed; though he is not much of a liberal, just a decent man
with only a limited appreciation of the political institutions
and practices necessary to uphold that public correlative of
private decency known as the rule of law. In this, he is a better,
and a sadder, representative than Adrian Leverkühn could ever
be of countless, equally decent, Germans who allowed themselves, without any sense of something as dramatic as a satanic

'pact', to become accomplices in wanton aggression and mass murder.

The idea of distinctive national characteristics has to be distinguished from the much less rational belief that nations as such possess personalities. This belief is prominent in the discussions Zeitblom records from Leverkühn's days as a somewhat marginal member of the Christian student corporation 'Winfried' at the University of Halle. Though these episodes are set in the first years of this century, most of the jargon churned around by the students as they hike through the countryside was culled from a pamphlet of the early 1930s which the author had been imprudent enough to send to Thomas Mann. (The gentleman concerned was not very good at learning from experience: some forty years after his first misjudgement, with Mann long since dead and buried, he saw fit to publish a denunciation of Mann's 'plagiarism'.) The assumption of all the participants, questioned only by Leverkühn, is that it makes sense to describe the German 'Volk' as 'young', and to interpret issues of national and international politics in terms of the alleged 'rights' of a 'youthful' nation. Leverkühn asks what meaning the term 'young' can have when applied to the German nation, except as sentimental drapery for certain prosaic historical facts:

I wish someone would tell me ... what it is that's supposed to make us so immature, so young, as you put it, as a nation. After all, we've been around for as long as the rest, and perhaps it's just our history, the fact that we were a bit late coming together and forming a sense of common identity, that misleads us into thinking we're particularly youthful.

These remarks, with their unemphatic, even tentative, manner, so far from the bombast of his conversation partners, are characteristic of Leverkühn's (admittedly rare) utterances on matters outside music. They help to indicate why the charge of 'arrogance' refuses to stick, since they show how inoffensively his intellectual powers are deployed, precisely when they are at their most penetrating. The retort (for it is far from being a reply) he elicits is notably different in terminology and syntax as well as in content:

'It's not like that at all', responded Deutschlin. 'Youth in the highest
sense has nothing to do with political history, nothing in fact to do
with history at all. It is a metaphysical gift, something rooted in
essential being, a structure and a destiny. Have you never heard of
German evolution, of the German as journeyman, of the eternal
quest of the German soul? ... To be young means to be original, to
remain close to the well-springs of life, it means rising up and shaking
off the fetters of an outworn civilisation, daring to do what others
lack the vital courage to undertake, that is: to plunge oneself into
the elemental.'   (p. 159, LP 119)

What was treated as deserving respect, even awe, when done
in the artistic sphere, namely the 'sinful' venture that purchased
'breakthrough' at a great personal cost, is seen here in the
political domain as a claim to hegemony and a pretext for
aggression, disguised maybe even from the speaker himself by
tiresome but tireless dead metaphors, all intent on obfuscating
political questions by casting them in bogus personal terms.

Not that the novel itself does not employ psychological
categories to illuminate historical forces. But whereas Deutschlin
and his associates psychologise Germany at the expense of
political insights, Mann lets Zeitblom evoke a particular
atmosphere, strongly tinged with collective neurosis, as the
manifestation (not the explanation) of underlying political
factors. The town of Kaisersaschern, where Zeitblom was born
and where Leverkühn spent his school years, is evoked as
an emblem of the spirit of Wilhelmine Germany. The town,
Zeitblom tells us, has retained 'something medieval' in its
appearance and atmosphere: 'the identity of the place asserts
itself against the current of time' (p. 51, LP 34). This is the
second example of a place apparently outside time that Zeitblom
has evoked. The first was the Leverkühn family farm, where
in every generation the elder son wanted to cut down the linden
tree in the farmyard in the interests of efficiency, only to defend
it in his old age in the cause of piety. But that timelessness
was presented as an unproblematic rural idyll (p. 19, LP 9),
quite unlike the phenomenon of 'a rational, prosaic modern
town' where there is nevertheless 'something in the air ... of
the mentality of the last decades of the fifteenth century ...
an element of a latent psychological epidemic' (p. 52, LP 34).

Here the apparent removal from the normal flow of time is an indication not of stability, but of lurking chaos. This is a continuity of precariousness, of hysteria beneath a thin veneer of normality. Kaisersaschern, unlike the Leverkühn's farm, is not outside the modern world, but its commitment to that world is half-hearted. While keeping up the appearance of normality, Kaisersaschern harbours forces subversive of rationality and order, though only as a hint or a threat, for it is too self-satisfiedly provincial ever to permit anything scandalous actually to occur: 'of course nothing happened, how could it have done? The police, in due accord with modern ideas of order, would not have allowed it.' Hysteria kept in check by police efficiency, in this formula Zeitblom attempts to catch a communal ethos easily capable of being transformed into something more overtly sinister once the police are ordered to 'keep quiet' at 'things which are a slap in the face for the spirit of modernity' (p. 52, LP 34). This 'spirit of Kaisersaschern' is extended in two directions. It is used to characterise Leverkühn and his works, the latter being described as 'Kaisersaschern music' (p. 113, LP 82), while the complex of inhibited desires which makes him so dramatically vulnerable to 'Esmeralda' can, Zeitblom suggests, be summed up in the single word 'Kaisersaschern' (p. 197, LP 149). At the same time, it is used to make a bridge between Leverkühn's psychology and the problem of German national identity, both of which are said to be marked by the strengths and weaknesses of a certain kind of monumental provincialism. This view is ascribed to the French–Jewish impresario Fitelberg, who tries in vain to bring Leverkühn and his characteristic music − 'c'est "boche" dans un degré fascinant' (p. 534, LP 410) − into the international limelight. He finds Leverkühn's rejection of his offer extremely 'German ... characteristically composed of arrogance and feelings of inferiority, of contempt and fear' (p. 539, LP 414). Zeitblom ascribes to Leverkühn 'a revulsion towards the Germanness which he embodied' − the same sentiment is attributed to the Holy Roman Emperor whose grave gives Kaisersaschern its name (p. 51, LP 33), and to Nietzsche in Thomas Mann's essay of 1947 (IX, 709) − and describes as symptoms of this revulsion 'the twin divergent manifestations of eccentric timidity towards the world and an inner need for a wider world' (p. 220, LP 167). At the other end of the link forged by 'Kaisersaschern', Zeitblom at the height of his 1914 enthusiasm suggests that German aggressiveness towards its European neighbours is an analogous example of over-compensation for feelings of inferiority, a resolve to conquer a 'world' which it fears it cannot win over by its merits:

> The most fundamental meaning of the breakthrough to world power to which destiny is calling us, is a breakthrough to the world itself, escaping from a solitude of which we are painfully aware and which no amount of healthy integration into the world economy since the foundation of the Reich has been able to shatter. The harsh thing is that it takes on the empirical form of a military campaign, when in reality it is desire, longing for union ...   (p. 409, LP 312–13)

These remarks elicit from Leverkühn the same sceptical response as the expatiations about German 'youthfulness' he heard in his student days, of which Zeitblom's words here remind him. Nevertheless, this psychologising of German foreign policy is not wholly disowned by the novel: the notion of Germany seeking international affection by force is linked to Leverkühn's psychology (whereas the claim that Germany has the characteristics of 'youth' is simply left hanging as a piece of rhetoric), which gives it a weight that shields it from Leverkühn's debunking. That does not, however, make it any more plausible.

Verdicts

Since *Doctor Faustus* is a reckoning as well as an account, it necessarily passes judgement on the Germany whose history it evokes. The verdicts are delivered by Zeitblom, whose qualifications to make them are enhanced rather than diminished by his more or less misguided youthful nationalism, which he has since learned to see in perspective. In his role of judge, as in the pattern of learning through experience and self-correction, Zeitblom is a recognisable image, though not a straightforward mouthpiece, of Thomas Mann. The judgement is complex, in that it considers fully, yet in the end rules out, mitigating circumstances such as the vulnerability of so many other European nations to fascism. The sense in which recent German history is said to be only a special case of a wider malady which Germany's defeat has by no means eradicated will be considered shortly, and it is one of the reasons why the interpretation of the novel as a comprehensive and exclusive denigration of Germany, widely held in the first years after its publication, is untenable. A more important argument against that interpretation is, however, furnished by a closer inspection of the terms on which Zeitblom most severely condemns Germany, for it emerges that, for all their high pathos, the passages concerned are anything but an indiscriminate vilification of all things German. The full weight of his condemnation is concentrated on two quite specific points: the repeated catastrophic failure of German political culture to master the use of power in the nation's true interests, and the monstrous crimes committed in the extermination camps. It is on these two issues, weighty enough to be sure, but by no means coterminous with the whole of German history, that Zeitblom, bringing his narrative to a close, can see only hopeless and irredeemable ignominy for his native land.

The first issue is impressed upon Zeitblom's attention by the implications of what he calls 'the devastating liberation' (p. 643, LP 497) which Germany is undergoing as the Allied troops advance into its territory, bringing to a disastrous end Germany's 'last and most extreme attempt to find a political form of its own' (p. 639, LP 494). He laments the fact that this liberation has, to the bitter end, to be enforced upon a people that seems incapable of freeing itself from obedience to a regime whose moral and military bankruptcy has long been obvious. What under one aspect seemed like a Wagnerian love of fate now appears, in the last months of the Hitler regime, to be a manifestation of a complete failure of political courage and will, quite devoid of any redeeming grandeur. Zeitblom's despair is heightened by the reflections forced upon him through the way his descriptions of the climate in Germany immediately after the end of the First World War coincide with the Allied liberation of France. The disaster of 1918 and the subsequent humiliations of the Treaty of Versailles were, he muses, trivial by comparison to what now awaits his country (p. 446, LP 343). Resentment against an 'alien' political form imposed by the victors was, Zeitblom recognises, an important factor undermining the Weimar Republic, a resentment he himself once shared. But now that Germany has once more, with unprecedented cost in human misery, made its neighbours 'shed their blood ... for the sake of German developmental processes' (p. 400, LP 306) he cannot imagine any other future for his country than complete submission to foreign control, an outcome as desolate and ominous as it is deserved. Germany in final defeat is envisaged as analogous to Leverkühn in his insanity; for all the patient's former qualities, he cannot be trusted to manage his own affairs and must be kept under tutelage for everyone's safety.

The judgements that aroused most indignation in Germany when the novel was first published are passed by Zeitblom in the specific context of the second issue which moves him to unqualified condemnation of his country: the mass extermination carried out in the camps, which we must suppose Zeitblom to have learned about through broadcasts like those Thomas Mann himself made via the BBC. It is in the light of such incomprehensible crimes that Zeitblom ponders whether Germany can ever again hold up its head among nations. His ruminations are cast in the form of questions leading up to a convoluted assertion about patriotism, hedged about with qualifications. The elaborate indirectness is not, however, meant to weaken the force of the indictment. In a text which has recorded many inflated expressions of narrow-minded or self-righteous zeal on 'national' issues, the tone of tentative musing is needed to vouch for the quality of the underlying conviction, its basis in harrowing clarity of insight:

Is it mere hypochondria to say that everything German, even the German spirit, German ideas, the German language are affected and made deeply questionable by these scandalous revelations? Is it morbid despondency to ask oneself the question how 'Germany' in any of its manifestations could ever in future dare open its mouth on humane issues? It may well be true that what has here come to

light are sinister possibilities of human nature in general – the fact
remains that it is German people, tens of thousands, hundreds of
thousands of them, who have perpetrated things that fill all mankind
with horror, and anyone who has ever lived in German [was nur
immer auf deutsch gelebt hat] stands exposed as a pariah and an
embodiment of evil.   (p. 638, LP 493)

Zeitblom then furnishes the link which allows him to connect
the restricted, though far from insignificant, number of
Germans who were directly involved in the extermination
programmes with his sense that in the post-war world Germany
will be 'a country that dare not show its face':

A patriotism that had the audacity to claim that the blood-drenched
state ... whose strident proclamation ... carried the masses along on
a surge of ecstatic happiness, a state under whose lurid banners our
youth marched with shining eyes, exuberant pride and firm faith,
to claim that this state was something wholly alien to our national
character, devoid of roots there, forced upon us – such a patriotism
I should have to judge to be more high-minded than honest.
                                                             (p. 639, LP 494)

Witnessing his friend's public self-condemnation on the
verge of dementia, Zeitblom reflected on the advantages of
'the protective non-committal character of art in comparison
with the crude self-exposure of unmediated confession' (p. 659,
LP 510). Like so many other comments in this novel, the remark
is also a statement about the text itself. In the face of the
indignation inspired in German readers by passages like those
just quoted (sometimes 'supported' by references to Germany's
rapid recovery of international standing after 1945), it is
essential to remember that they are indeed couched in the
'non-committal' guise of a single character's opinion, embedded
in a precise fictional location in time and space. They are the
expression of a complex personal response, not a political
forecast, still less an advocacy of any particular policy on the
part of Germany's victors. All too aware of what he had been
spared by his reluctant exile, Mann left the words of condemnation to a persona whose right to judge in this way must be
assessed by the correspondence between his opinions and his
represented experience. That experience, encompassing as it

does Zeitblom's manifest love of those values and traditions which he finally associates with Germany's descent into barbarity, lends Zeitblom's verdict as much weight as any fictional utterance can carry.

The movement of the times

Very many elements of the novel, from the allegorical basis of the parallel between Leverkühn and Germany through to the countless citations of themes from German culture and history, support the claim that National Socialism was something distinctively German. But that claim is embedded in a further contention that developments in twentieth-century Germany are a special case of a much wider pattern. The chief vehicle of this broader analysis are Zeitblom's reflections on the conversations he witnessed in intellectual circles in the early 1920s. He interleaves his account of these discussions with an exposition of Leverkühn's *Apocalipsis cum figuris*, composed at the same period, and he finds that both the discussions and his friend's work call forth similar reflections and disquiet. Whether in the culture-babble at the salon held by the Schlaginhaufens, an elderly couple with obviously ample private means, or in the more earnest debates within the circle presided over by Sixtus Kridwiß, a graphic designer who 'without any identifiable ideological commitment, kept out of pure curiosity an eager ear open for the way the times were moving' (p. 481, LP 369) the theme of the discussions which Zeitblom recounts is essentially that of Leverkühn's *Apocalipsis*: 'The end is nigh'.

Uniting Leverkühn's creative labours with cultural debates in which he personally takes not the slightest interest is what Zeitblom describes as

a sense that an epoch was coming to a close, an epoch that encompassed not only the nineteenth century, but reached back to the late Middle Ages, to the breaking of scholastic bonds [Bindungen], to the emancipation of the individual, the birth of freedom, an epoch which I was obliged to acknowledge as in the widest sense my true intellectual home, the epoch, in short, of liberal humanism.

(pp. 468–9, LP 359)

At many levels, the novel attempts both to evoke and to validate this 'sense of an ending' and to offer it as the fundamental explanation for the political and social events of European history in the first half of the twentieth century. Here as elsewhere when it is a matter of historical commentary, Zeitblom offers the same kind of analyses as we find in Mann's writings *in propria persona*. The links which are asserted between German history and wider developments are anchored in the notion that the trauma of defeat in the First World War gave Germany 'a certain intellectual lead over [other countries]' (p. 484, LP 372) an earlier and clearer perception of the signs of the times:

> No wonder then, that [this sense that an epoch was ending] dominated people's minds more decisively in a devastated land like Germany than in the victorious nations ... They in no way perceived the war as the deep and definitive historical caesura which we saw in it, but simply viewed it as a disruption which had been happily overcome, after which life could resume the course from which it had been forced to deviate. (p. 469, LP 360)

Zeitblom records that he 'envied' the French the 'justification and confirmation' that their liberal mentality had received 'to all appearances, at any rate' through victory (p. 469, LP 360). But the qualification 'to all appearances' indicates that this 'justification' is illusory. The course of events in the later 1920s and beyond, Zeitblom believes, proved that the German insight was correct by exposing the frailty of liberal institutions all over Europe. Zeitblom identifies three claims being made by the intellectuals whose discussions he witnessed. To the conviction that liberal humanism has had its day − their first main point − they add the argument that an alternative philosophy from which social and political principles can be derived is urgently required, and an assertion that this new philosophy should be one of totalitarian rule grounded in a mixture of mythological propaganda and collectivist terror. Nothing, either in Zeitblom's analyses or elsewhere in the novel, offers any serious resistance to the first two of these positions. The intellectual structure of the novel is built upon an unquestioned belief that a radical and comprehensive cultural crisis is the prime feature of contemporary Western history; and the idea that the solution to that crisis must lie in finding what the wandering students once described as 'the right bond' (die rechte Bindung) (p. 161, LP 121) that can furnish social and political cohesion after the alleged collapse of liberalism is one that unites every voice cited and implied within the text. Only when it comes to identifying what that 'right bond' should be do Zeitblom and his creator signal divergence from the proto-Nazis and their hangers-on.

The core of the critique which the novel levels against Weimar intellectuals, then, is that they were too eager to draw the wrong conclusions from their conviction that liberal humanism and its associated political values belonged only to the past. It does not take issue with that conviction, indeed it shares and helps propagate it, and that is its most abidingly problematic feature. Here is Zeitblom in 1944, explaining why (again, like his creator) he flirted with Bolshevik sympathies after the collapse of the monarchy in 1918:

The Russian revolution affected me deeply, and the historical superiority of its principles, compared with those of the powers which had us under their heel was in my eyes beyond doubt. Since then history has taught me to view our erstwhile conquerors, soon to conquer us once again, with different eyes. True enough, certain circles within liberal democracy seemed, and still seem today to be ripe for what I have called rule by the dregs of humanity – willing to ally themselves to it to prolong the retention of their privileges. Nevertheless, democratic leaders have arisen who ... saw in that rule the worst evil that could be visited upon mankind ... and stirred up their people to a life and death struggle against it. No thanks can be too great for these men, and they prove that Western democracy, for all the historical outdatedness of its institutions, for all the stubborn refusal of its conception of freedom to recognise the new and the necessary, nevertheless does lie on the path of human progress, of the honest will to perfect society, and is essentially capable of being renewed, improved, rejuvenated, translated into new forms more appropriate to life.   (p. 452, LP 347)

According to this, both the 'principles' and the 'institutions' of liberal democracy are outdated, and it has a conception of freedom that refuses to recognise 'the necessary'. This points towards an understanding of history as a teleological pattern within which the political values of the French and American revolutions have now played out their part. The general character of history is 'human progress' and the end goal is the 'perfection', no less, of society. Presumably the 'new' and 'necessary' things against which liberal democracy 'stubbornly' turns its face are notions of freedom which restrict individual self-realisation in the interests of larger social concerns. Though too fuzzy to be confidently categorised, these ideas allude to a marxist understanding of history. Distinctly un-marxist, however, is the last phrase, where Nietzsche's most elusive and protean criterion for value-judgements, 'life', is brought into play as the standard by which the closeness of a social order to the true path of progress is to be judged. The appeal to this idea allows Zeitblom to round off his paragraph in a reassuring fashion: after all, if history, the honest pursuit of human progress and 'life' itself are all heading for perfection, there would seem to be little grounds for long-term anxiety about the future of mankind. The consoling conclusion does not, however, do much for the internal coherence of his ideas.

Beyond all the novel's directly theological allusions, such political analyses as it offers turn out to have a highly problematic religious dimension in the sense of the (speculative) derivation of 'religion' from re-ligere, to bind up again. It claims that modernity involves fragmentation, isolation, and disintegration which must in the longer term prove beyond human endurance, leading people to seek refuge in some sort of 'bond', for better or – as Germany's example has shown – very much for worse. Zeitblom's position seems here identical with Mann's own, as it is expressed in his writings of the immediate post-war period, where he is fond of saying that after the 'end' of bourgeois liberalism, the nations of the world, victors and vanquished alike, have only the choice between fascism and socialism. Attempts to sustain the 'historically outdated' principles of liberal democracy in their 'Western' form, so the implication runs, will simply invite further adventures in the direction of fascism. Only a turn towards socialist forms of political organisation can fulfil the need for 'Bindung' which modern emancipation has heightened by neglect. This view would be simply a matter for political debate rather than literary critical analysis, were it not so firmly located in the assumption, shared by fascism and many forms of socialism alike, that politics really is about the solution of personal crises of identity and purpose. To do full justice to the appeal of totalitarian doctrines in the twentieth century, that assumption itself needs to be challenged, something which Thomas Mann in his middle and later years consistently failed to do. For all his ignorant dismissal of politics as a demeaning business unworthy of higher beings, the Thomas Mann of the *Reflections of a Nonpolitical Man* had one important insight that he later lost until his very last years, after *Doctor Faustus* was completed: an understanding of the folly of expecting politics to meet distinctively private, let alone religious needs. The terms in which *Doctor Faustus* attempts to judge fascism as a threat to modern societies imply a wish that is as chimerical as it is seductive: the longing for forms of association capable of securing not simply material prosperity but richness of experience; not only due process but integrity of being; not merely justice, but justification. And since that longing is itself part of the totalitarian malady, this novel, a fascinating symptom rather than a telling diagnosis, offers little hope of a remedy.

Chapter 5

Reception

A climate of resentment

On 31 August 1949 an item appeared in the *Frankfurter Rundschau* and a number of other German newspapers which will have a familiar ring to observers of the end of the GDR:

> The town council of Marktredwitz has resolved in open session by nine votes to eight that a street named after the writer Thomas Mann should be renamed Goethestraße. A spokesman for the council, explaining this measure, said that since the war ... Thomas Mann had behaved with a lack of piety towards his German fatherland. He was blatantly devoid of true inner culture [Herzensbildung] and his lack of friendliness towards Germany had left the council no other choice.

Such antics in a Bavarian Titipu would hardly concern us, were it not for the glimpse they provide of the rancorous climate in which Thomas Mann in general, and *Doctor Faustus* in particular, were received in defeated Germany. For received Thomas Mann certainly was: a study by Gerhard Roloff, *Exil und Exilliteratur in der deutschen Presse 1945–49* (Worms, 1976) shows that, in a representative selection of newspapers and periodicals published in Germany in the first five post-war years, Mann was mentioned much more frequently than any other exiled artist or intellectual. Roloff's results for the ten most frequently mentioned names merit presentation in graphical form (Figure 1). Equally revealing when charted are Roloff's figures for the distribution of press references to Thomas Mann across the five-year period (Figure 2). The high figures for 1947 and 1949 coincide with Mann's two trips to Europe, and with what were in effect the two publication dates of *Doctor Faustus* (see below). These trips and their public repercussions are inextricably bound up with the German reception of the novel, making it hard to separate public reactions to the novel itself from the wider issue of Mann's standing in the Germany of the immediate post-war period.

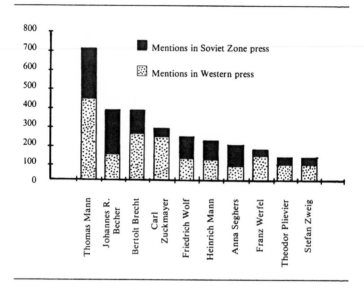

Figure 1. Mentions of exile writers in a sample of German press, 1945–9.
Data from Roloff, *Exil und Exilliteratur*.

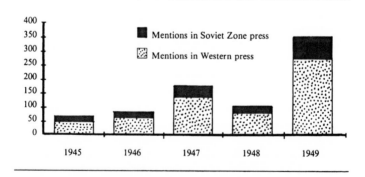

Figure 2. Mentions of Thomas Mann in a sample of German press, 1945–9.
Data from Roloff, *Exil und Exilliteratur*.

There is a further complication in the way of evaluating early opinions about the novel. When zealots descend on a complex work of fiction, there is always the suspicion that few of them have bothered to read what they condemn. That suspicion is compounded in the case of the early publishing history of *Doctor Faustus* by the fact that there were virtually no copies in circulation in Germany when the controversy reached its first peak. The initial printing of some 14,000 in October 1947 was distributed mainly in Switzerland. It was not until early 1949 that Suhrkamp in Frankfurt brought out an edition for the German market, and even then with a first run of only 7,000. (By this time over a quarter of a million copies of the English translation had been printed in the USA, the numbers swollen by its choice as the Book of the Month Club's offering for November 1948.) The reviewer of *Doctor Faustus* for *Die Welt* (31 January 1948) prefaced his piece with a plea to readers not to ask to borrow his copy, since it was only on loan to him; and Hans Mayer, demolishing a history of literature which claimed to cover Mann's latest novel, roundly accused the author of deception. 'He hasn't read the book. It's simply not obtainable here' (*Neue Zeitung*, 12 December 1947). Reading what purport to be judgements about the text, one can never be sure how far the novel is being used, unread, as a pretext for praising or (more frequently) castigating Mann's whole career since the 1920s.

The controversies which so obscure the novel's reception began while it was still being written. In an open letter of August 1945, Walter von Molo, who had been President of the literature section of the Prussian Academy of Arts until 1933, invited Thomas Mann to return to Germany and join in the rebuilding of German culture. Mann explained his unwillingness to accept the invitation at that juncture in conciliatory tones, but his refusal unleashed an unsavoury barrage of resentful commentary from representatives of the self-styled 'inner emigration', anxious to portray themselves as heroic sufferers under Hitler's regime in contrast to the those who had taken the allegedly easy and cowardly path of abandoning 'their sick mother Germany', in one participant's nauseating phrase. Mann's first post-war European trip on the eve of the novel's publication in 1947, which took him, among other places, to both Holland and Switzerland, gave offence by its studious avoidance of German territory. But he caused even more outrage when he eventually did visit his native country in 1949, for he insisted on making public appearances in both the Western and the Soviet zones, precisely at a time when the die had been cast for the creation of the two ideologically opposed states.

What singled Mann out for vituperation by the lugubrious apologists of 'inner emigration', quite apart from *Doctor Faustus*, was a simple fact to which his whole biography testified: he was living proof that it had been possible for a conservative-minded observer, steeped in a love of 'German' values, to see the true nature of National Socialism and draw appropriate conclusions, long before Hitler came to power, let alone by the time his regime was established. Other émigrés, communists or Jews, were disqualified in conservative eyes as judges of German values and so presented less of an embarrassment. That meant that Thomas Mann's opposition to National Socialism had to be rendered suspect, to be portrayed as a by-product of a depraved mentality. He had condemned Hitler, so the implication ran, not because he had perceived his evil intentions, but because he would have rejected any and every advocate of truly German interests, evil or not. Hence the repeated claim in early German reviews of *Doctor Faustus* that the novel expresses comprehensive and impious hatred of all things German, past, present and to come. Wearisome debates from the early decades of the century over the distinction between the 'Dichter' − the truly 'poetic' artist − and the 'Schriftsteller' − the mere intellectual scribbler − are revived to support the claim that Thomas Mann is quite simply incapable of understanding his subject-matter. 'It was hardly to be expected that a mind [Geist] like Thomas Mann's could have written the sort of work that Germany really needs', commented Hans Paschke, publisher of the conservative periodical *Merkur* in 1949, trying at one and the same time to write Mann off as spiritually defective and blame him for failing in his patriotic duty. Another commentator, writing in a periodical edited by Alfred Döblin, a fellow exile who had always intensely despised Thomas Mann, claimed that the novel's 'horrendous oversimplifications' were 'monstrous deeds [Untaten] fully on a par with political atrocities'. No one said in so many words that there must after all be something to be said for Hitler if a degenerate like Thomas Mann disapproved of him, but one suspects that only Allied supervision kept this sentiment from coming to the surface.

Critical beginnings

Academic criticism of the novel started with an essay by Erich von Kahler, 'Die Säkularisierung des Teufels' (The Secularisation of the Devil), *Neue Rundschau* 1948, a philosopher Mann knew from his time in Princeton, whose access to sections of the novel in manuscript gave him a head start on other scholars. His thoughtful, if occasionally rather breezy account of the novel's secularising tendency − Mann himself declared it 'magnificent' (XI, 250) − provoked one strand of the invective against Mann by Hans-Egon Holthusen in 'Die Welt ohne Transzendenz. Eine Studie zu Thomas Manns *Doktor Faustus* und seinen Nebenschriften' (World Without Transcendence. A Study of Thomas Mann's *Doctor Faustus* and its Associated Writings), initially in *Merkur* 1949, then in book form in the same year. Despite its author's subsequent reputation as a literary critic, Holthusen's essay is hard to distinguish in its main thrust from the whingeings of the reviewers. On Holthusen's account, Mann's secular outlook deprives him of the ability, maybe even the right, to interpret German history and culture, and lies behind his alleged wholesale vilification of all things German in the novel.

Another early critic whose treatment of *Doctor Faustus* was less impressive than his general reputation might have led one to expect was the Austrian marxist Ernst Fischer. Despite his advocacy elsewhere of an aesthetic free from the trammels of Stalinist orthodoxy, his discussion of Mann's novel, '*Doktor Faustus* und die deutsche Katastrophe. Eine Auseinandersetzung

mit Thomas Mann' in *Kunst und Menschlichkeit,* Vienna
1949 (*Doctor Faustus* and the German Catastrophe. A Critical
Examination of Thomas Mann) leaves little to be desired as an
example of crude application of the tenets of socialist realism.
Initial praise of the 'masterpiece' becomes faint indeed as we
find that it engages in mystification by focussing on Leverkühn's demonised subjectivity and leaving aside the workers
on the one hand and the Junkers and business tycoons on the
other, without whom the true nature of National Socialism
as a late capitalist phenomenon cannot be grasped. Another
distinguished marxist critic, Georg Lukács, did the novel much
more justice in his 'Die Tragödie der modernen Kunst' (The
Tragedy of Modern Art), first published in Hungarian in 1948
and contained in the collection edited by R. Wolff listed in the
suggestions for further reading, below. Though often mocked,
justifiably enough, for trying to harness the novel to Soviet
campaigns against modernist music, he also offers an intelligent
account of Mann's attempt to locate fascism in a wider cultural
and historical context, providing the first reasoned refutation
of the accusation that the novel was 'anti-German'.

It was not until some time after Mann's death that native
Germanistik began an adequate engagement with his works,
Doctor Faustus included. An adequate survey of the tendencies
that ensued is beyond the present study, but the works listed
in the suggestions for further reading provide some indications
for the interested reader.

Creative influence

The cultural caesura brought about by the defeat of Hitler's
regime and the full exposure of its atrocities meant that for
writers emerging after 1945, Thomas Mann's themes and devices
seemed to belong to a remote age. This helps explain why his
works, *Doctor Faustus* included, have left virtually no trace in
the creative writing of post-war Germany. When other, much
younger novelists of comparable stature (Günter Grass in *Die
Blechtrommel* (1959), Christa Wolf in *Kindheitsmuster* (1976))
made their attempts to encompass the power of National

Socialism within fiction, they did so in ways that could and did
derive nothing from Mann's example. The resolute attempts
of Hannelore Mundt in her *'Doktor Faustus' und die Folgen*
(Bonn, 1988) to trace the presence of Mann's novel in several
post-war writers by a series of what amount to *lucus a non
lucendo* arguments serve in the end only to reinforce the judgement that he belongs to a world with which contemporary
creative sensibilities find it hard, if not impossible, to engage.

The novel has, however, left its mark in the cinema. In
addition to a film version by Franz Seitz (1981, documented
in a volume *Doktor Faustus. Ein Film von Franz Seitz nach
dem Roman von Thomas Mann*, edited by Gabriele Seitz,
Frankfurt am Main, 1982) which has seldom been shown outside
Germany, Visconti's celebrated recreation of *Death in Venice*
(1971) draws extensively on *Doctor Faustus*, as is signalled
by the opening shot of the boat taking Aschenbach to Venice,
which bears the name *Esmeralda* on its stern.

Trouble with 'the real one'

On his seventieth birthday in June 1945, Mann received from
Schoenberg the manuscript of a canon with a dedication
expressing the hope that they would long remain 'gute Zeit-
genossen' (good contemporaries), a slightly odd phrase which
was doubtless cordially meant. The wish was not to come true.
Mann sent Schoenberg a copy of his newly published novel
inscribed 'Arnold Schönberg, dem Eigentlichen' ('to Arnold
Schoenberg, the real one'), only to learn that the composer
had taken umbrage at the version of the novel conveyed to him
by Alma Mahler-Werfel, who seems to have been intent on
stirring up trouble between her two 'friends' whilst officiously
pretending to mediate between them: Schoenberg, who had
eye problems, may never have read the book himself. He was
above all worried that future generations might think that his
theory and technique of twelve-tone composition were actually
the invention of Mann or his fictitious character. On learning
of this concern, Mann attempted to meet it by ensuring that the
English translation and all later German editions bore a note

stating that the twelve-tone technique was 'in reality the intellectual property of a contemporary composer and theoretician,
Arnold Schoenberg'. Mann was too much of an ironist to resist
beginning the note with a remark that its inclusion did 'not
seem superfluous', but it was not that phrase which raised
Schoenberg to new heights of indignation. In a huffy letter to
the *Saturday Review of Literature* (1 January 1949) Schoenberg
revealed that what rankled above all was an indefinite article:

> [Mr Mann] added a new crime to his first, in the attempt to belittle
> me: He calls me '*a* [a!] *contemporary* composer and theoretician'.
> Of course, in two or three decades, one will know which of the two
> was the other's contemporary.

Mann, who was capable of extreme touchiness himself, refused
to be provoked and remained unfailingly conciliatory and considerate towards Schoenberg. Early in 1950, Schoenberg wrote
to Mann stating that their quarrel was over, though he refused
to say so in public on the curious grounds that this would let
down his supporters in the unilateral dispute. Though most of
Schoenberg's complaints are silly enough, there was a grain
of truth in his sense that his reputation with posterity was at
stake. On several occasions, Mann remarked that precisely
because so much of Leverkühn was drawn from Nietzsche,
Nietzsche himself could not figure within Leverkühn's intellectual horizon. What he probably overlooked was that the
same was *a fortiori* true of Schoenberg. The decision to make
Leverkühn invent twelve-tone composition necessarily meant
that in Leverkühn's world, Schoenberg simply could not be
allowed to exist. Mann was forced to invent a censored version
of musical history, which could retain Wagner, Brahms,
Mahler, Debussy, Ravel and Richard Strauss (along with Otto
Klemperer, Bruno Walter, Desiderius Fehér, Eugene Ansermet
and the Donaueschingen Festivals of New Music), but had to
exclude Schoenberg and his associates. It is hard to avoid the
suspicion that Schoenberg, had he indeed read the novel, would
have been still more deeply offended, and with good reason: to
find oneself written out of history in the interests of a fictional
construct can hardly be a pleasant experience.

Suggestions for further reading

Primary text

The standard edition of Mann's works in German is *Werke in 13 Bänden* (Frankfurt am Main, 1974), containing both prose fiction and essays. An overview of his voluminous, and frequently repetitious, correspondence, published in many separate collections, is provided in H. Bürgin and H.-O. Mayer (editors), *Die Briefe Thomas Manns, Regesten und Register*, 5 volumes (Frankfurt am Main, 1976–87), and his diaries (parts of which have upset people who think that great writers must be great-hearted) have been edited by P. de Mendelssohn and I. Jens, *Thomas Mann. Tagebücher*, 9 volumes (Frankfurt am Main, 1979–93). All his fictional works, mostly translated by H. Lowe-Porter, are available in English translation: the edition of *Doctor Faustus* in the Everyman's Library series (London, 1992) has a succinct introduction by T. J. Reed. Also available are the *Reflections of a Nonpolitical Man*, translated by W. D. Morris (New York, 1983), an anthology of *Essays of Three Decades*, translated by H. Lowe-Porter (London, 1947), a selection of his Wagner writings as *Pro and contra Wagner*, translated by A. Blunden and introduced by E. Heller (Chicago, 1985) and (of particular interest to readers of *Doctor Faustus*) *Thomas Mann's Addresses, delivered at the Library of Congress, 1942–1949* (Washington, 1963). R. and C. Winston have translated a selection of *The Letters of Thomas Mann* (Harmondsworth, 1975) and his *Diaries for 1918–1939* (New York, 1982). Readers with no German who wish to sample Nietzsche's thought can consult *A Nietzsche Reader*, selected and translated by R. J. Hollingdale (Harmondsworth, 1977) and *The Portable Nietzsche*, selected and translated by W. Kaufmann (New York, 1976). Adorno's *Philosophie der neuen Musik* is available as *Philosophy of Modern Music*, translated by A. G. Mitchell and W. V. Blomster (New York, 1984).

Bibliographical aids

Leaving aside exhaustive catalogues mainly of interest to specialists, there are helpful surveys of criticism and scholarship in: H. Lehnert, *Thomas-Mann-Forschung. Ein Bericht* (Stuttgart, 1969); H. Kurzke, *Thomas-Mann-Forschung 1969–1976. Ein kritischer Bericht* (Frankfurt am Main, 1977); and V. Hansen, *Thomas Mann*, Sammlung Metzler (Stuttgart, 1984). An excellent combination of a study of the

106 *Suggestions for further reading*

primary works and the main currents of scholarship is provided by
H. Kurzke, *Thomas Mann. Epoche-Werk-Wirkung* (Munich, 1985).

Biographies

Only the earlier part of Mann's life is covered by the most authoritative
and detailed German biography: Peter de Mendelssohn, *Der Zauberer.
Das Leben des deutschen Schriftstellers Thomas Mann: Erster Teil,
1875–1918* (Frankfurt am Main, 1975). The author has since died,
so no further volumes will appear. The most detailed biography in
English covers a similar period, and likewise will remain without a
sequel due to the author's death: Richard Winston, *Thomas Mann.
The Making of an Artist, 1875–1911* (London 1982). Briefer and
with a broader compass is Nigel Hamilton, *The Brothers Mann. The
Lives of Heinrich and Thomas Mann 1871–1950 and 1875–1955*
(London, 1982). The details of Mann's life year by year are provided
in Hans Bürgin and Hans-Otto Mayer, *Thomas Mann. A Chronicle
of his Life*, translated by Eugene Dobson (Alabama, 1969). The
German original, *Thomas Mann. Eine Chronik seines Lebens* (Frankfurt am Main, 1965), was reprinted in paperback with some corrections
in 1974.

General books on Thomas Mann

The English-speaking reader is well served by a range of general
introductions, of which perhaps the most useful are: R. Hinton
Thomas, *Thomas Mann. The Mediation of Art* (Oxford, 1956);
A. White, *Thomas Mann* (Edinburgh, 1965); J.P. Stern, *Thomas
Mann* (New York, 1967); I. Feuerlicht, *Thomas Mann* (New York,
1968); R.J. Hollingdale, *Thomas Mann. A Critical Study* (London,
1971); M. Swales, *Thomas Mann. A Critical Study* (London, 1980)
and M. Travers, *Thomas Mann* (London, 1992). Two of the finest
specialist studies are also in English: Erich Heller, *The Ironic German.
A Study of Thomas Mann* (London, 1958, third edition Cambridge,
1981) and above all T.J. Reed, *Thomas Mann. The Uses of Tradition*
(Oxford, 1974). Readers with knowledge of German should consult
the *Thomas-Mann-Handbuch*, edited by H. Koopmann (Stuttgart,
1990), a compendium of essays by distinguished scholars which provides an excellent introduction to current Thomas Mann studies.

Studies of *Doctor Faustus*

(a) In English
Here, too, the reader with no German has access to a good range of
works. In addition to chapters on *Doctor Faustus* in all the books

listed in the previous section, there are two studies of the Faust
tradition which consider Mann's novel at some length: E. M. Butler,
The Fortunes of Faust (Cambridge, 1979), and J. W. Smeed, *Faust in
Literature* (London, 1975). The latter author's *Don Juan. Variations
on a Theme* (London, 1990) is also of interest, since it explores some
of the connections between the Faust and Don Juan stories. Patrick
Carnegy, *Faust as Magician. A Study of Thomas Mann's 'Doktor
Faustus'* (London, 1973) is especially valuable for its consideration
of the musicological aspects, and there is a wealth of insights in J. P.
Stern's 'History and Allegory in Thomas Mann's *Doktor Faustus*'
(Inaugural Lecture, University College London, 1973).

(b) In German

Two books bring the resources of the Thomas Mann Archive in
Zürich to bear upon the novel: L. Voss, *Die Entstehung von Thomas
Manns 'Doktor Faustus'. Dargestellt anhand von unveröffentlichen
Vorarbeiten* (Tübingen, 1975); and the second edition of G. Bergsten,
*Thomas Manns 'Doktor Faustus'. Untersuchungen zu den Quellen
und Struktur des Romans* (Tübingen, 1974). The first edition of
Bergsten's book (Stockholm, 1963), pre-dating full availability of the
archive material, is available in an English translation by K. Winston
(Chicago, 1969). A good selection of Mann's own remarks about his
novel can be found in H. Wysling and M. Fischer (editors), *Dichter
über ihre Dichtungen. Thomas Mann*, volume 3 (Zürich 1981), and
the controversies surrounding the novel's first appearance are
documented in K. Schröter (editor), *Thomas Mann im Urteil seiner
Zeit. Dokumente 1891 bis 1955* (Hamburg, 1969). Interesting essays
from a variety of standpoints can be found in R. Wolff (editor),
Thomas Manns 'Doktor Faustus' und die Wirkung (Bonn, 1983);
and H. Lehnert and P. C. Pfeiffer (editors), *Thomas Mann's 'Doktor
Faustus'. A Novel at the Margins of Modernism* (Columbia SC, 1991),
and the chapters on the novel in the following studies of Mann are all
thought-provoking: I. Diersen, *Thomas Mann. Episches Werk −
Weltanschauung − Leben* (Berlin, 1975), pp. 304−84; H. Jendreiek,
Thomas Mann. Der demokratische Roman (Düsseldorf, 1977),
pp. 412−91; E. Hefterich, *Vom Verfall zur Apokalypse. Über
Thomas Mann* (Frankfurt am Main, 1982), pp. 173−288; and H.
Koopmann, *Der schwierige Deutsche. Studien zum Werk Thomas
Manns* (Tübingen, 1988), pp. 79−124. Among the many specialised
monographs on particular aspects of the work, the general reader will
find much of value in Hans Wisskirchen, *Zeitgeschichte im Roman.
Zu Thomas Manns 'Zauberberg' und 'Doktor Faustus'* (Berne, 1986).

Historical/cultural background

The accounts given in conventional political histories are not always easy to relate to Thomas Mann's writing. Readers looking for an understanding of the broader issues behind the cultural movements in which Mann is chiefly interested are referred to V. R. Berghahn, *Modern Germany. Economy and Politics in the Twentieth Century*, second edition (Cambridge, 1988); J. P. Stern, *Hitler. The Führer and the People*, third edition (London, 1990); and Mary Fulbrook, *The Divided Nation* (London, 1991), pp. 1–128. For Adorno's ideas, see D. Held, *Introduction to Critical Theory* (London, 1980) and D. Kellner, *Critical Theory, Marxism and Modernity* (Oxford, 1989).

LaVergne, TN USA
23 May 2010
183694LV00001B/95/A